A CALL AT DOWN
A Message From Our Brothers of The Planets Pluto and Jupiter

Kelvin Rowe

Non-Fiction

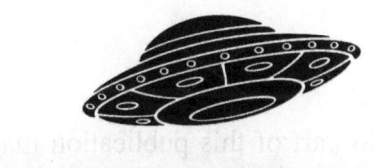

SAUCERIAN PUBLISHER
Original Sources in Ufology

ISBN: **978-1-955087-38-4**

© 2022, Saucerian Publisher

Al rights reserved. No part of this publication maybe reproduced, translate, store in a retrieval system, or transmitted in any form or by any means, electronic, mechanical, photocopying, recording or otherwise, without prior written permission from the publisher.

Kelvin Rowe

Prologue

Kelvin Rowe is not as generally well known as other contactees but was a frequent lecturer in the 1950s and 60s. He lectured at the Giant Rock Spacecraft Conventions 1957-1959. Rowe was born in Chicago, Illinois, on March 14, 1908, but would move with all his family to Los Angeles, California, where his mother had gotten a job at the Hollywood Sanitarium, as a nurse and obstetrician. He attended high school (Virgil Jr. High School) and from there left to work as a truck driver. "My mother wanted me to be a doctor or an electrician, but like most children I was the opposite of what my mother wanted me to become.". The family moved back to Good Hope Acres, near Lake Elsinore, where Kelvin got a job at a Safeway grocery store, and then was again hired as a trailer driver to travel between Los Angeles and Texas.

In the times of the Great Depression, he was employed as a Senior Clerk and Time-keeper. Then he returned to his love of trucks, working for his older brother. In 1940 he worked for the International Union of Operating Engineers as a heavy equipment operator. There, in 1948, he met the contactee Truman Bethurum. In 1954 he entered the California State Forestry Division where he ended up retiring.

The story and experiences told by Kelvin Rowe are in general the same as the other contactees. But Rowe was interested in flying saucers before his first contact and had met George Adamski and Truman Bethurum already in 1953. The first experience was by telepathy on March 9, 1954, as described in his book: "I was on my way to San Bernardino, Calif., driving a Ford pick-up. I was thinking I would visit a friend of mine in Redlands on my way home, when the word Pluto popped up into my mind and was repeated three times. The words that followed were not too distinct at first, evidently due to my inexperience with and lack of understanding of the use of mental communication."

After eight months of many mental communications, Rowe had

his first physical contact with two the ""Brothers". "They were fine looking men, with smooth, dark sun-tan complexions, and dark hair styled in longer length than our modern cuts… The iridescent material of their form-fitting garments, similar in style to our ski-suits, was unusually soft to the touch, firm but beautifully textured." After this first contact he met the space people frequently, either at home or was taken up in their space craft. According to Rowe he encountered both men and women and most of them came from Jupiter and Pluto. Also, Rowe mentioned that sometimes encountered the visitors, dressed as ordinary earth people, mingling in society. He also claims to have been taken to Mexico in their craft as well as below the oceans. In *A Call at Dawn* is mentioned that: "Our Brothers are operating on an entirely different frequency or spectrum than we are here as third dimensional beings".

The message from the space people, as presented in *A Call at Dawn*, is in general the same as coming from other contactees. However with one marked difference. Kelvin Rowe was deeply involved with the Brotherhood of the White Temple, situated in Sedalia, Colorado, founded by Maurice Doreal, (aka: Claude Dodgin).

Rowe claimed to have doctor's degree from the *Brotherhood of the White Temple,* and this gave him the right to teach philosophy and metaphysics. He pointed out this it's not a scientific degree of any kind. Also, he claimed his book that the space people suggested he study the material from this brotherhood. They even "approved of it as being the highest source of Truth teachings aviable in the Western Hemisphere."

A Call at Dawn was dedicated to "Mr. George Adamski through whom I was led to realize the true reality of interplanetary visitors; and, to Dr. M Doreal whose teachings have shown me The Way". It deals specifically with the communication of aliens from Pluto and Jupiter, claiming that they are our brothers.

Saucerian Publisher was founded with the mission of promoting books in Science Fiction. Our vision is to preserve the legacy of literary history by reprint editions of books which have already been exhausted or are difficult to obtain. Our goal is to help readers, educators and researchers by bringing back original publications that are difficult to find at reasonable price, while preserving the legacy of universal knowledge. This book is an authentic reproduction of the original printed text in shades of gray and may contain minor errors. Despite the fact that we have attempted to accurately maintain the integrity of the original work, the present reproduction may have minor errors due to the conditions of the scanned copies. Because this book is culturally important, we have made available as part of our commitment to protect, preserve and promote knowledge in the world. 'This title was originally published in 1958.

Editor
Saucerian Publisher, 2022

I DEDICATE THIS BOOK
TO THE WARRIORS OF THE DAWN

I extend my deepest appreciation to our Brothers and Sisters of other planets to whom I am humbly grateful for their guidance and friendship; to Mr. George Adamski through whom I was led to realize the true reality of interplanetary visitors; and, to Dr. M. Doreal whose teachings have shown me The Way.

MOTTO

"No knowledge is forbidden to man when he has by his own efforts, made himself ready to receive: so he who has ears to hear, let him hear."

CONTENTS

		Page
Foreword		11
Definition of Frontispiece		19

Chapter

1.	The Awakening	25
2.	Time of Trouble	32
3.	I Meet the Space People	41
4.	Cosmic Cycles	59
5.	Into Cosmic Light	73
6.	Cause and Effect	86
7.	Peace	99
8.	Conquest of the Skies	107
9.	Why Don't 'They'?	118
10.	Visit With the Brothers	131
11.	Aboard the Ship	151
12.	Few Are Chosen	168

Addenda 190

What The Brotherhood of the White Temple Teaches 197

The experiences related herein are based on my contacts prior to and up to March 1956, and not on contacts henceforth.

ILLUSTRATIONS

	facing
Frontispiece	*Title*
Emblem of Jupiter	22
Cruiser Ship	145
Emblem of Pluto	120

FOREWORD

"He that refuseth instruction despiseth his own soul; but he that heareth reproof getteth understanding."—Prov. 15: 32

I am quite without what is conventionally called education. I have been told it was not intended that I should have, for academic education does not manifest spiritual and intellectual humility, but more often than not it fetters and binds, and acts as a 'block' to a higher understanding of life. My education did not really begin until 1954.

My background is an unpretentious one; my life has been an ordinary one. I was born in Chicago, Illinois, March 14th of the year 1908, the seventh member of the family. At the age of four, my mother and her children moved to Hollywood, Calif. Being a nurse and obstetrician, she established and operated the Hollywood Sanitarium for assisting women in childbirth. I grew up in the Los Angeles-Hollywood area and quit school after attending the ninth grade at Virgil Jr. High School. I then acquired a truck-driving job for myself. My mother wanted me to be a doctor or electrician, but like most children I was contrary to what mother wished me to become. When I was about sixteen, mother moved to Good Hope Acres in the country. I spent many happy days swimming and boating at nearby Lake Elsinore, during which time I miraculousy escaped drowning in a whirlpool. I was later employed for a time in a Safeway grocery store, and after that drove freight-line between Los Angeles and Texas. I did not escape The Depression unscathed. During WPA (Works Progress Administration) I was employed as a Senior Clerk and Timekeeper. Succeeding this job I went to Los Angeles and drove truck for my brother, later joining the Operating Engineers in 1940. I worked under their jurisdiction as heavy-equipment operator until four years ago when I sought and received employment with the State of California Division of Forestry in 1954.

In the early part of 1953 while working at Iron Mt., California, my life was again miraculously spared. The difference this time being that a Voice spoke to me. Nearly a year later I realized my first contact via mental telepathy with the Space Men. Seven and a half months after my first mental communication I had my first objective contact, person to person. About five months afterwards I rode the great spaceways at a rate of speed that defies all imagination.

There you have my life history all in a nutshell, and for the most part an uneventful one up until 1953. No doubt you are wondering why I have been contacted by people from other planets. At this time I can only reveal that it is due to a Cause set up in a past incarnation.

I do not expect you to take my narration for granted, but in reading it may you do so with diligence, weigh it and consider, and taste well thereof, failing not to read between the lines. I fully realize that many are not ready to accept such a story as mine as one of fact, and will only scoff at it, but no individual's personal opinion will alter the truth. Personally, I shall not feel badly if you choose to remain a skeptic, for everyone is free to believe or disbelieve. On the other hand, I know that there are those who are seeking and who are ready, and will therefore find that special spark of truth herein that will cause their dim, inner flicker of 'light' to kindle and glow like a candle, and grow ever brighter. It will glow in the dark and the light will banish that darkness.

Undoubtedly there will be those who feel that I have done nothing but find fault with my people. If I condone my fellow-men in their mistakes then I help to strengthen the condition. I have pointed out the things that are detrimental to their progress, knowing that in trying to explain the truth in the world that I'll 'get it in the neck' from every direction. I have spoken in the nature of reproof that the unawakened may be alerted to the true condition of man's existence today, and realize that inherently man does not desire destruction or to wage wars, but is driven by his fears, and therefore, we must become more concerned with the Creator and His Divine Laws than we are concerned with man-made laws. We do not necessarily need repudiation of present religions, but a realization of the one true religion—that taught by Jesus, the Christ, to his disciples.

I am aware that beings of other planets are clear out of our realm of limited thinking—that is for most of us—which means it is difficult to accept them or their words of wisdom. But they are among us—in the fields of science, in government circles, in all walks of life, quietly guiding those few willing to make this a better world. Unbeknown to men of Earth they have, the past several years, rendered indispensable service in many ways, without which we undoubtedly would not be here today. They know that in the beginning, mankind did not learn his lesson, and since has denied the things of spirit, failing to serve his Creator, and instead, consciously or unconsciously trying to be a creator, without knowing the power he is exercising. They stress that we do not understand the nature of the Creator and that we lack this understanding because of the shackles of tradition and belief which we must cast off, and in place establish spiritual freedom. It is most important that we become aware of the godlike potentials within ourselves.

Man, walking in darkness, needs guidance and counsel through the Time of Trouble. The tremendous upheaval and disorder is fast approaching in which man will be hopeless in his own power. The Bible tells us. "Satan will be loosed for a little while before being bound." In a short while he will be loosed upon the face of the Earth, and great calamities will befall man that will bring him to the point where no longer will the material have value to him. Already the dark forces of the anti-christ are being marshalled against the forces of the Prince of Light. Turn not your back upon this day, but take your rightful place, having absolute faith there is a plan which will raise man out of his limitations, and fear not, for the forces of Light will triumph over the forces of darkness. We are entering the final days before the emergence of the World Savior, when the Christ Consciousness comes in the flesh to the entire world. Only when all people in the world are brought into oneness of purpose will the Christ Kingdom manifest in the world, and mankind know the beauty of peace and brotherhood.

Yes, dear reader, I know it seems very hard that mankind must pass through chaos. Yet we must remember that God gave man the power to manifest that which he wishes, and so he was not compelled to do it, but did so by his own actions, and today he reaps his harvest. He feels the affects of his own causes.

Throughout the long Ages man as a mass has futilely

struggled against the force of negation, but passing along the road of darkness he enters that path from which he sprang. At last the victory he has longed for is at hand, and an ordered, peaceful world lies ahead.

I leave with you the following verse from Romans 12: 2, "Be not conformed to this world: but be ye transformed by the renewing of your mind, that ye may prove what *is* that good and acceptable will of God."

The Author

THESIS

"Accept thy brother and sister from the land—
The Creator will give thy hand.
   Learn thyself from the heart—
   The Creator will do thy part.
You will then know Nature and become free;
You will know what to do when you come to Thee."

ACKNOWLEDGEMENTS

All quotations unless otherwise stated are taken from material printed by the BROTHERHOOD OF THE WHITE TEMPLE, INC.

Since the Brothers of our sister planets have informed me that the teachings of the BROTHERHOOD OF THE WHITE TEMPLE are universal and the highest source of Truth available in our Western Hemisphere, I am indebted to the BROTHERHOOD OF THE WHITE TEMPLE for underlying ideas and principles used throughout this book in explaining some of the many things told to me by the Brothers from outer space.

THE ALPHA AND THE OMEGA
(Definition of Frontispiece)

In the beginning (ALPHA) before any creation began, there was only the ONE (LIGHT). The Light cast out from its perfectness all of the disorder which is also itself, and thus is symbolized as the darkest of the Light.

The Inner Light became the most perfect—the Outer Light non-perfect, or ORDER and DISORDER. When this disordered light became so intense it started pressing inwardly towards the ordered Light of PERFECTION, this movement set up a CAUSE which later brought into material manifestation, motion, rhythm, vibration, etc., which became the manifestation of the Divine Wisdom, known to man as GOD.

The CROSS is a symbol of the Primary Laws by which God created, symbolical of the four winds, of North, East, South and West, of the nine dimensions, and of the four planes on which man manifests.

The CIRCLE represents ALL of CREATION, the whole of Infinity. Outside of the Circle there is only the Void, or non-creation.

The EYE is symbolical of God, LIGHT OF DIVINE WISDOM, from whence all creation came into manifestation.

The DOUBLE TRIANGLE symbolizes the SPIRITUAL and MENTAL manifestations through which the world and man were brought into being.

The SEVEN RAYS symbolize the seven days in which God created the Worlds, and represent the SEVEN CYCLES or ages a planet passes through before attaining perfection. In reality there are more than seven rays but they are beyond the normal comprehension of the mass consciousness.

The NEW AGE our planet has now entered is symbolized by the rising SUN. Man in this New Age is confused, and must decide which of the two paths he will travel—the RIGHT HAND PATH or the LEFT HAND PATH. If he chooses the right path, he shall walk through the Archway that leads step by step to the portico of the Temple of the Holy City. If he chooses the wrong path he will become chained to the negation of his own making.

Man, having been imbued with the SPARK of DIVINE WISDOM, can, by his own WILL, break the chain that holds him a prisoner to this negation.

It is said that in the beginning the Atom or SOUL UNIT which is man, was created equal. What Man Is Today Is Of His Own Creation, and Equality Has Ceased To Be. But the time will come when man will

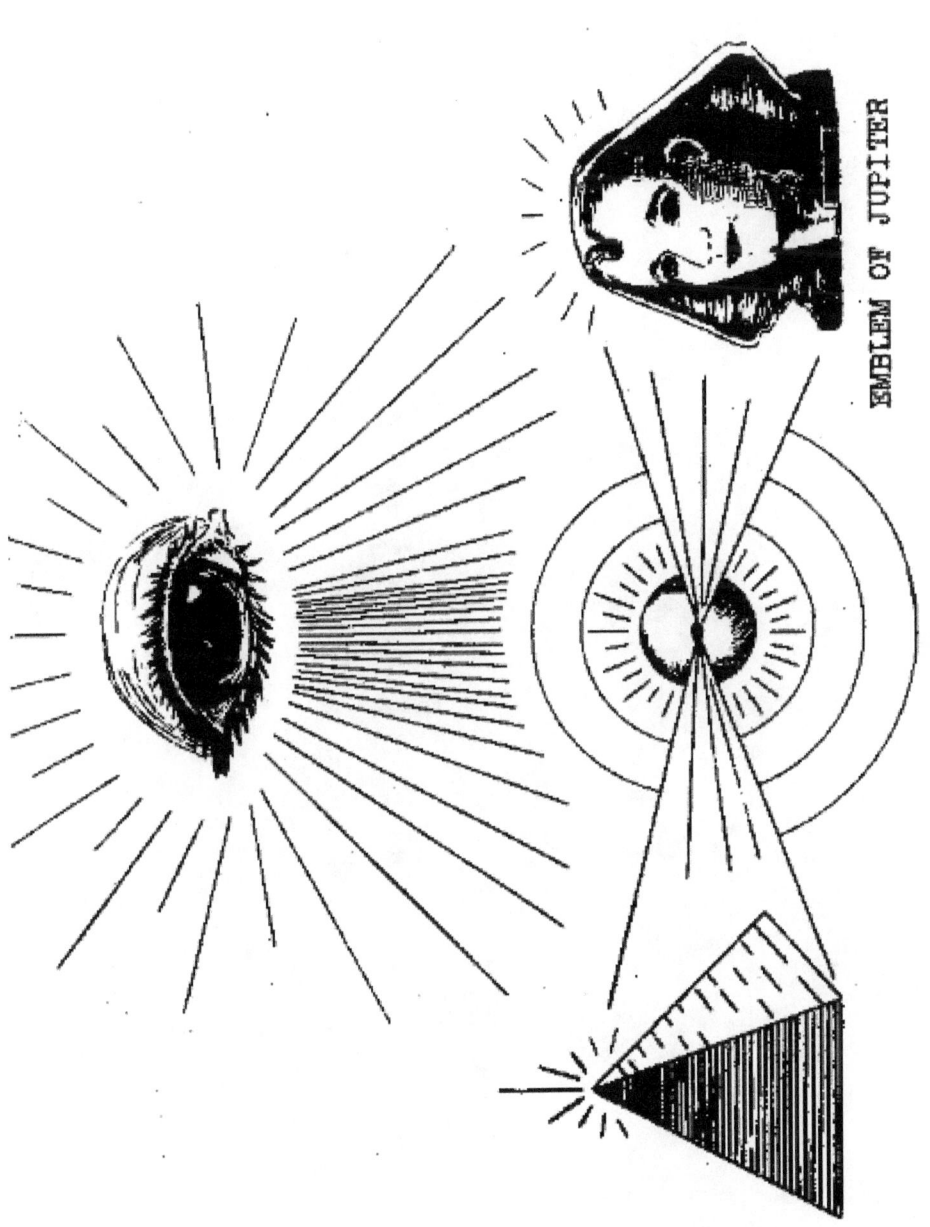

emerge *into full realization of what he is, of his own true nature*—changing disorder into order, creating perfection in himself and his surroundings as was originally intended, until at last he brings forth the establishment of THE CHRIST KINGDOM ON EARTH, for this planet and MANY like it are all moving towards that state in which the manifestations of consciousness on them will be linked in ONENESS and HARMONY through the DIVINE WISDOM and POWER called God.

In the end (OMEGA) man will have reached his goal—ONENESS with the CREATOR; he will have returned from whence he came!

—*M. Swift*

The theme of this frontispiece is one example of Cosmic Art which will undoubtedly become the trend in the field of arts in the ensuing Spiritual Age of Man. It is an art that is genuinely realistic as it seeks to reveal the basic, triple realities of nature, mind and the Creator. It is a symbolic synthesis of man's most monumental feelings which express that spiritual quality so lacking in the multitude of present day artistic works.

Chapter One

THE AWAKENING

A New Age has dawned, and there is an Awakening throughout the World. The Earth is presently undergoing a new initiation, a period in which "All Things Are To Become New!" Space is fast becoming a new frontier, and the yearning to travel to some far off planet is perfectly natural for all thinking people, for we are not just children of Earth, we are children of the Universe; we are a part of the Cosmos, physically, mentally and spiritually. Yet we have been quite unaware of this fact, never giving it a serious thought, being limited in a knowledge of The Whole.

Uncounted millions of people throughout the world, living their superficial lives, going about their daily tasks, seldom step out into the night and pause for even a moment to lift their eyes and fill with reverential contemplation or thrill with inexpressible wonder at the glory of the heavens. Because of our beliefs, the Creator and his vast realms are little understood; they have merely been taken for granted. In our false concepts of life and the Universe, we have selfishly held, though not admittedly, that the stars, the sun and the moon all shine for us alone. Our understanding has been so narrow, our understanding of ourselves so little that when confronted with the possibility of life like ours existing on any other planet, we have raised our voice in derision, crying out, "No one lives but us!" Poor, puny little human beings, living in bondage to and dwelling in darkness on a 'speck of dust'* spinning through the far reaches of God's unlimited Creation, believing ourselves to be super-men, yet incapable of traveling the great space-ways to far, distant and remote lands. We disdain to contemplate denizens of other planets, lest we be confronted with greater powers than we can answer to, lest we find we are not a super-race after all. All this notwithstanding, there is an undercurrent, a spiritual quickening, a restlessness over the Earth.

Indeed, among men of this world there has been much controversial discourse as to whether or not the beings designated as spacemen, or people of other planets, really exist. By scientific theory the world has long been informed that there cannot possibly be life, as we know it, on other planets in this system or in other systems. But, in the first place, theory really proves nothing, and scientists are recognizing that

---

* Planets can be said to be 'specks of dust' because they are merely great coalesced masses of Cosmic Dust imbued with energy, and passing through long periods of growth in the great infinity of space.

yesterday's theories apply only to yesterday, not to today or tomorrow. In the second place, such denial is blasphemy, for it is limiting the Creator in His Infinite completeness.

There are those of us who know the truth that inhabitants of other worlds are among us, coming and going, having learned our ways and fitted themselves into our society so that they are inconspicuous, for too many people yet disbelieve there are other human beings outside the realm of the planet Earth. It is urgent that certain truths must be given to the world through contactees who are willing to serve. We have been in contact with them person to person in the physical, these meetings having nothing whatever to do with spiritualistic, psychic, or supernatural phenomena. When I say 'there are those of us,' I refer, too, to those of officialdom in the various governments of this Earth, who have been contacted, but as yet refuse to make any public admission. Skepticism and ridicule are partly the reason for their silence.

I tell you plainly that these people of other planets live and have their being just as you and I, and are fundamentally no different. The apparent difference lies in that they have a deeper understanding of the Cosmos, and are more highly evolved in comparison to us, mentally, physically and spiritually, having developed from bondage into freedom—freedom from bondage of life in the darkness of Illusion; freedom from bondage to a human body; freedom from bondage to their respective planets. By this, I mean that to them there is no death as we know it. To them it is progress from one life to the next. And they are not bound to their planets for they are free to travel interplanetary, having gained the knowledge and wisdom that has given them the efficiency and the power.

Therefore, I say to you, begin now to think, for thinking is a creative process. Has it not been the breaking away from old accepted beliefs of mankind that has brought all the advancement in knowledge man of Earth has ever had? Is is not to those who had the courage to study and learn the truth, regardless of what others believed, that we owe all that we have today that makes this a better world to live in than it was centuries ago? Remember, there is no end to knowledge, and though for the past ten years man has not advanced spiritually one iota, spiritual advancement now lies before him. Man's thinking needs spiritual activity, for man is not only a material being but a spiritual being, and the attainment of true spiritual knowledge is one of the most important things in his life. Indeed, if mankind is to survive and progress to higher levels, a new way of thinking is essential. It is the only way to divert coming disaster in his life, for the battle between the forces of darkness and light is under way whether man has yet become aware of it or not. Nevertheless, thinking people are beginning to realize that we of Earth must learn and submit to the truth that harmony and peace are more desirable than destruction.

Let us turn back the pages of the calendars to a day in the early part of 1953. To begin my story I can only mention a miracle* that saved my life. It was a miracle at that time because I did not clearly understand what had happened. My lack of knowledge veiled the truth that was waiting to unfold into reality, then it would no longer be a magic mystery to me. I dared tell no one for I was certain that to anyone else it would be a ridiculous impossibility, and besides I had pledged a promise to the Creator on this occasion. Months rolled by, the miracle locked within my heart, not even my family knowing how close I had come to departing by transition, and never had any light been shed on it that would explain it.

Later in 1953, and through my eldest daughter's profound interest in a most remarkable person she had seen and heard at Palomar Gardens Cafe in 1952 when my sister had stopped there on a Sunday drive, my family and I went to meet Mr. George Adamski, a pioneer of a new frontier—Outerspace. He has blazed a trail of truth for all to follow who will. We listened

---

* Miracles: the wonderful things that happen to us are not miracles in the ordinary definition of the word, but the working of infallible laws we do not understand.

to this crusader of the New Age speak of interplanetary ships and people of our sister planets, and strangely enough this possibility did not seem at all impossible. We accepted most all that he said with scarcely a doubt. Perhaps you'll concede that we were being too gullible, but this was no little thing to be lightly tossed aside. This was something that seemed to be so much a part of our deeper selves that no argument served to move it. 'Twas as if this were something we had long known, like a memory so far off it seemed pigeon-holed in the dim recesses of the past, and it was now being recalled for us. From then on we were frequent visitors at the Gardens, friends often accompanying us. It was as though a magnet drew us there again and again, and we were intellectually hungry for more knowledge of this vast subject men of Earth dubbed 'flying saucers.'

Each individual who is actually in contact with people from other planets has a given duty to perform in service to mankind and to the Creator, being free to accept or reject it. Each duty as it is fulfilled will ultimately complete a picture which now seems to be a jigsaw puzzle—it will be the most wondrous picture man has ever beheld with mortal eyes.

Mr. Adamski's greatest task as a selected emissary on this Earth has been to alert our present civilization to the seriousness of our world's situation and to warn of the vast peril we face, of the change that is taking place in this solar system, that we may help ourselves and our fellow men. Other practical men, also with their feet on the ground, have been quietly striving to find some way to avert coming disaster, and have found none. In turning back the pages of history it appears that man has proven his total incompetence to direct and govern himself other than by destructive means. Two thousand years of wars, books and sermons, yet the world knows no peace. The solution lies within the heart of man—man, whose paramount and most urgent need is guidance and counsel from beings of higher authority, knowledge and wisdom, who can well assist us out of the chaos into which we are slipping, for no scientist or political or religious leader has yet devised a formula to show us how to live together in peace. There are men who are seeking; there are men crying out for God and peace and they are not finding either.

Chapter Two

TIME OF TROUBLE

During 1953 and through a tape recording Mr. George Adamski had played for us, I became reacquainted with Mr. Truman Bethurum, then of Redondo Beach, California, who had had several contacts with a scow from the planet Clarion. I had first met Mr. Bethurum in 1948 when we were both employed on a construction job under the jurisdiction of the International Union of Operating Engineers. Now, when he returned to Overton, Nevada, in the anticipation of a promised twelfth contact, and due to our mutual interest in Flying Saucers, he invited me to join him. It was through the interference of others, the detail of which I shall omit, that his hoped for contact did not occur at this time. However, after months of long waiting, his faith in a promised return was, he has now disclosed, rewarded in December 1955.

I will add that while in Overton, and due to observing too strictly custom and social convention of our Earth people, I, too, missed a contact. No one told me that I had missed, but deep within my being I felt it.

After returning home I called on Mr. Adamski, and without my having so much as mentioned this feeling to him, he made a flat statement out of a clear sky, with a twinkle in his eyes, "So you missed your contact while in Nevada." He never explained how he knew, but my hunch was confirmed.

I suppose I should have been greatly disappointed that I had missed, but the disappointment I did experience was not long endured, and as the days passed by, my interest in Flying Saucers never waned. About four months later and on the ninth of March, 1954, a strange incident occurred. I was on my way to San Bernardino, Calif., driving a Ford pick-up. I was thinking I would visit a friend of mine in Redlands on my way home, when the word 'Pluto' popped into my mind and was repeated three times. The words that followed were not too distinct at first, evidently due to my inexperience with and lack of understanding of the use of mental communication. However, at that time I did not realize what was actually happening. I only knew that it recalled to me that miracle early in 1953 when a voice had solaced me. It is said by our Earth people that there are such beings we call 'guardian angels.' There are various opinions as to what or whom a guardian angel may be. How unbelievable it may seem that they are no different from the most humble soul that walks the Earth, other than being richly imbued with a consciousness of Cosmic Laws and of pleasing the Creator or Supreme Intelligence, and carrying out His will.

The sensation of high vibration* that accompanied this experience left me no little perturbed, lasting the greater part of the day. On my way home I was in doubt whether or not to relate this incident to my wife, not being certain what she might think. But I was glad that I told her for she was of the opinion that it was not anything to be alarmed about, but rather a happy occasion, for she believed I had had a contact, and that it would probably be wise to talk to Mr. Adamski about it.

A few contacts and five days later I went to Mr. Adamski for advice. He assured me I had been contacted, but absolutely not by any spirit:** that the sensation that accompanied the contact was due to the high frequency of the space-man's thought. Thus began a series of contacts by telepathic impression or thought transference. I was informed that I was receptive and, indeed, I was given ample practice, being

---
*"Vibration is the controlling factor in every object or thing throughout the entire Universe, and the Universe is ruled and regulated through vibration. The law of vibration is regulated by rhythm."

** "Some so-called spirits manifested by mediums are nothing else than the elemental entities [of a vibration consolidated into manifestation through the medium of ectoplasm] who assume the voice or form of loved one, to deceive the seeker into laying himself open to obsession or possession. Their sole purpose in deceiving is to gain confidence so that they can open the seeker to their entry. In mediumistic practices there is great danger of Soul bondage."

assured that everything would be clear to me in time. These people, our Brothers, *feel* their every thought, and so poignant is that feeling that you are impregnated with it, too. Their messages are always closed with blessings and love, and it is impossible to convey by the written word the impressiveness expressed by them.

Then the day finally came when I had presumedly progressed in receptivity to the degree that I was ready to be contacted clairaudiently or by the inner voice which was distinctly audible as though someone were present and conversing with me, yet, at the same time, it was as if it originated in the brain or the inner ear. Anyone sitting next to me would not necessarily be aware whatever of such communication, for when a higher dimension is realized by the awakened mind, as is the case with our Brothers of other planets, thoughts and words can be sent around the world at a rate of speed that transcends what we consider the speed of light, and they are heard by those for whom they are intended.

Although it has been proven by scientific tests that such power as mental communication exists, it is not only one of the strangest phenomena in the world, but we are not able to define the law under which it manifests. Yet such communication is a common thing with people of other planets who have developed thus far by "attuning the inner man to the Cosmic and becoming channels for the magnetic force of the universe."

When we speak of telepathic communication we must recognize that man has two separate and distinct minds, the objective and the subjective. All communications must take place between the subjective minds, whatever part may or may not be taken by objective minds.

The whole human body is a magnet in as much as it has two polarities, and every person possesses magnetism in either latent or active state. The magnetic force of each person vibrates in a certain octave or vibration, and it is upon this magnetic force that telepathic thought is conveyed when directed by the will to the person you are directing it to. Thought is of high electrical content, and the sender and receiver must be attuned to the same mental vibratory wave length, for harmony and attunement of minds is the first requisite for mental communication from one brain to another. The human will is the director of the magnetic current; the magnetic current is the carrier of thought, and is capable of almost unlimited extension when properly directed by the will. Communication may take place between persons in the same room or thousands of miles apart, and at any time.

In a greater or lesser degree, magnetism, a vital force of a fine electrical nature, radiates from every human body, and since each individual has his own particular rate of vibration he can be attuned accordingly, much as you turn the dial of your radio to the frequency or wave length of the desired station, for two minds in attunement are sending and receiving stations. I was not capable of attuning my mind to that of the space-man, but for him, having that understanding of the more subtle energies and the ability to use them, it was a simple thing to attune his mind to mine that he might commune with me.

Here I wish to point out that when continual contact is necessary with a mind of a much lower vibratory wave length than his own, a space-man can use a sending and receiving instrument which acts as an intermediary, raising or lowering the vibrational rate of the thought waves of the sender or receiver to the same unified frequency, making it possible for the two minds to communicate. That is, the instrument intercepts the mental message sent out from a mind of a low vibrational scale, multiplying the frequency into the high octave of vibration needed to reach the space-man's mind, thus conveying the message to him. Also the process is reversed, the instrument acting as a step-down frequency transformer, converting the high vibration to the lower rate required for attunement. This particular instrument is used to eliminate any detrimental effects that a continual lowering of one's state of consciousness could cause. Conceding a low vibration to be non-constructive, we should strive to cast our thoughts ever upward into the higher rates of vibration, into freedom of Light, Love and Life. Then, too, by thus raising the state of our consciousness we can meet our Brothers of other worlds on a level and harmonize with them.

These Guardians of Space, our Brothers, are continually doing all they can in many ways to benefit mankind, although they could do much more if this were not a quarantined world. i.e. This mediator type instrument is not only employed for individual contacts, but to send thought impressions to untold numbers of people. Many are unknowingly benefited in this manner, the instrument being adjusted to transmit within a given area, positive and harmonious thoughts, relayed in a specific octave of vibration. Anyone within that given area whose vibratory wave length is somewhere within that certain range of vibration will receive some of these impressions. If one's frequency should be synchronized to the entire octave in which the thoughts are transmitted he would receive all of the contributory impressions.

It is possible to use this equipment for mind impingement; that is, to direct thought impressions to an individual not capable of normal reception, compelling him to speak aloud the impressions sent to him. But this is *never* done for negative purposes, but *always* for the highest good. Yet, suppose that rulers of a nation on this Earth, ruling supreme over all other nations, came into possession of similar machines and used them with evil intent, forcing the people to bow down beneath their reign like robots.

Let us refer to the Book of Revelation, Chapter 18: 16-17-18.

Verse eighteen has aroused more controversy than almost any other verse in the Bible. The number of the beast is the number of man, not a man; the 'a' being an interpolation. The number 666 is the vibratory number of the octave of vibration along which man's thought travels. The basic vibratory thought octave of mankind is 666 million millions. In other words this is a universal thought octave of all mankind. Each and every man, forced to submit to an operation, would have individual connection or vibration, along which this universal thought octave can travel, and would have its corresponding or like vibration in a machine, which would also be stamped with his individual number or mark. The ruling council would direct at will the actions and thoughts of all subjects attuned to the tiny machines in the great scientific laboratories.

This could very well come to pass while the antichrist is in power. There is more than one faction trying to influence the minds of men in order to rule them. It has already been announced over TV that Russian scientists have made a successful experiment, inserting a tiny box into the brain of a human being, thereby controlling his every thought and action. All this depicts a frighteningly possible near-future under totalitarian thought control in which there would be no room for things of the spirit. Man, through the law of Cause and Effect, has brought negation into his world, and he must combat and remove it. Without question he has now entered into the Time of Trouble so often written of and so long prophesied—Armageddon.

We are now being confronted with turbulent conditions preceding the final terrific struggle of the Battle of Armageddon. During that final phase the antichrist will be dominant, great changes will take place on the Earth's surface, and one-half or more of the population may be destroyed as foretold. Only the righteous shall stand; those in the Light will survive. Signs and portents are all about us by which we might know what to expect, and our Brothers of neighboring planets are proffering their assistance.

No peace parley, nor council of men or nations however powerful, will ever prevent war, destruction and chaos. We must recognize that man has an unrestrained, destructive principle in his being. There is only one thing to be done and that is to remove the cause for destruction which lies in man's selfishness, in his desire for power over his fellow man, and in the lack of a consciousness of brotherhood. Man seeks not the Kingdom of Heaven *first!* The responsibility of bringing about such a removal of negation begins first with the individual and next with all leaders of all governments and all religions on this Earth.

Chapter Three

I MEET THE SPACE PEOPLE

During a mental telepathy contact on the twenty-fourth of March, 1954, I declared that "I would like to meet you in person some place."

The response was, "You will in time; you may not know when you do." And so it was.

A Space Craft Convention was to be held for the first time on the fourth of April, 1954, at Giant Rock, near Joshua Tree, California. I had not considered going, and it was not until the late afternoon of April the third, while visiting friends, that the Convention entered into the conversation, and we decided to attend. We left early the following morning.

On arrival I joined Mr. Truman Bethurum and spent most of the day in his company, never giving any special thought to being on the alert to spot my "friends" should they be present. So, completely unaware of it at the time, I met three of them, a young lady and two gentlemen. They approached Mr. Bethurum and inquired about his contacts in Nevada, just as any number of other folks had been doing all morning. However, up to the time of this interview I had not entered into the conversation or been in any pictures that were taken of him. Now, however, I was asked to step up and have my picture taken with him, as well as being questioned about my visit with Mr. Bethurum in Overton, Nevada. The 'cards' in a manner of speaking, had been 'laid on the table face up,' but I overlooked the 'jack in the pot' at the moment I should have 'trumped it.' How did these perfect strangers know I had been in Overton with Mr. Bethurum since he had not mentioned it to them or to anyone else he had spoken with? In the late afternoon on rejoining my wife we were quite inclined to suspect that both of us had met them, though not at the same time.

This experience of meeting them without realizing it disclosed to me that it is profitable to be alert, else one can miss a great deal in life. The man who is ever observant is the one who gains the greater knowledge and understanding. It is according to man's capacity to become aware that he grows slowly or rapidly in consciousness. If he is not aware or conscious of a thing it does not exist for him for he is separated from it, and the less he is aware of, the smaller the world he dwells in.

These three extra-terrestrials from the planet Pluto mingled with the crowd at The Rock, undistinguishable, so like us they are, and no one recognized them or was in the least suspicious of their identity. Yet, unquestionably, practically everyone there was anticipating thrills and excitement and waited expectantly to see a space-being stand out conspicuously in the crowd like a wart on the nose of creation, garbed in unusual raiment, a bulbous-headed freak with bulging eyes and queer features. However, a true seeker would have quietly searched for very different qualities in the person he might suspect of being from another world.

Our meeting with them at the Convention was later verified by a message received by the inner-voice, for the first time, which registered upon my inner-ear. The voice was of a pleasing tone quality, clear and distinct, and disclosed, "You know by this time you have met us. You did not recognize us. Your wife, though very observant, met us when she least expected it."

I now took the opportunity to ask if it was so that women of Earth are not contacted, and why? Our Sister from Pluto, whom I shall henceforth refer to as The Lady of Pluto, informed me that this question had been asked of them before, and that it would not be answered until the proper time. From this one gathers that there is a time for the ebb and a time for the flow, a right time and place for all things as well as a reason for all things.

She did explain that by the laws and customs of men on our planet Earth, women have long been looked upon unfavorably as the weaker sex and unfit for men's work, and men have been considered the leaders, but, that women are the stronger by far, and that there would be little difficulty preparing the women to do their part in improving world conditions. As time goes on more women will have professional careers, and more authority in our government, holding high political offices which will result in changing some of our present laws and thereby helping to avoid much destructiveness and conflict. She went on to say they contact the men because men of our governmental and scientific world will not fully accept our women, heed or pay attention to them. Most of our scientists will be difficult to teach because they will not humble themselves and begin all over on the foundation that the basis of all science lies in the control of the laws of vibration. This is not to say that the entire fabric of science need be discarded in order to begin all over. It is that she indicated our scientists are going to have to reconstruct every scientific theory, and become cognizant of immutable law that governs the Universe and to which man must eventually conform. Not one premise concerning the structure of matter is based on fact, but what has been learned through experience should be utilized as a stepping stone to a broader field of knowledge and wisdom, at last establishing a firm bond between man and the nature the Creator gave him.

I also inquired on this occasion if I might meet them

personally and visit their space-craft. The response was, "You are not to be impatient. When the time is right you will be contacted in person—you may board our craft. There is much studying to be done; much work to do." At this time I did not even slightly perceive of the magnitude of their reference to study and work. Ever before us is work to be done.

I have learned that you merit such a privilege as a contact. All that we receive comes to us through an immutable process of Divine Law. We bring into our lives the fruits of our actions and thoughts. We earn the right by becoming worthy of each honor bestowed upon us. Nothing is handed out to us on a silver platter. We must make an effort, then we will be rewarded accordingly. If man had been given all things without effort on his part he should have been robbed of the whip of necessity, and would have stagnated rather than developed to the position where he now stands.

Next I inquired as to what I might do to be of service and was given to understand that I would be directed, that "we are all working as One with the Creator." I was referred to Mr. George Adamski as my advisor, and directed to hold group meetings as "people of Earth must know more about people of other planets." It was also suggested at this time that I should not persuade anyone to attend the meetings— let them know. For "there is no soul that should not have the opportunity to advance and learn the Truth. Any one individual should not be restrained because another is not ready to advance. Such a person should be put aside until the time is right for him to accept the Truth."

The group meetings began with a good attendance though comprised mostly of curiosity seekers and skeptics, and they dropped out one by one and a few at a time, until only a handful of true seekers were left. My helpers and I felt no little chagrin, until our Brothers comforted us with, "Only a few are on the right path. You have not failed where many others have; your efforts have not been casted." There is an upsurge, a great will among only a limited number on this Earth, for the elimination of negation from their lives and for a greater knowledge of man, his life and relationship to the vast Universe in which he dwells. There are other key groups all over the world, quietly working, and meeting regularly with no public fanfare, each group varying in size as to number of followers.

Our Brothers suggested that I study. I had been reading material published by THE BROTHERHOOD OF THE WHITE TEMPLE, INC., and they approved of it as being the highest source of Truth teachings available in the Western Hemisphere. When I enquired if I should direct my group to the same source, they assured me, "There are no better teachings. The people of Earth should study and understand the laws of Nature and the ways of the Creator. They should learn to love the Creator, and attain a happier way of life."

This work is like a torchlight held high in the darkness, for it is untampered by scheming clergy bent on power. In it those desiring deeper insight, those who wish to be workers of the New Age, will find a plan of action by which to help prepare the way for a new and better world emerging from the ruins of the old. Unlike most teachings, it has an applicable system whereby one may grow in knowledge and attainment, gaining an understanding of himself and his fellowman. ("Attainment does not mean eternal rest, but rather an opportunity and ability to do more and greater things.") Since the majority of religions are circumscribed and considered to be "all the truth and there is nothing that can be added and nothing that can be taken away," I desire, unpretentiously, to propagate this one teaching in particular, Ancient Wisdom, a Cosmic teaching. It is not my intent to imply that there are no other worthwhile teachings, for there are other orders and brothers, each in their own way becoming channels, either knowingly or unknowingly, through which the Divine may manifest. But despite what we may have chosen to study we should not confine ourselves to a limited knowledge of the planet Earth alone but to an over-all understanding of the Cosmos—of the whole.

In gratitude to our Brothers, and filled with humbleness and gladness, I share this treasured advice with you, dear reader, that you may, if you are ready, enter upon the Path of Light. Our Brothers, the Guardians of Earth, referred me to this particular teaching because it concerns Cosmic and Universal Law and its relation to man. The messages of Ancient Wisdom will help regain the Spirituality that was our original heritage before the Fall of Man—help us set our goal and attain our Oneness with that power we call God.

You may question, and rightly, why we should be concerned with anything so ancient as Ancient Wisdom teachings. Remember that:

> "All the concepts of God that the modern Christian has are derived from the ancient Teachings, the source and the God were the same. When speaking of ancient records I am not talking about the ancient books of history that the average man has access to, because the literature of the ancients has in part been destroyed or lost to modern man. As an example, the hundred and five books of history of ancient Rome rest today in the Vaults of the Vatican because it is not well for people to know too much! These ancient records reveal too much of the pre-history of mankind and of things that upset the old accepted theories of science and theology.
>
> It has always been the policy of certain institutions and organizations in the world to destroy or hide knowledge. It has always been the policy of others to preserve it. The books of secrets have been

restrained from the public. We can get references by studying the ancient works that are available but the *real* things have always been hidden from the mass of people. Throughout the ages past the mysteries were not a mystery to those who were worthy to receive them. If asked why this knowledge of man, his destiny and his potential powers has been concealed and reserved for the few—we shall answer and say that the acquisition of all forms of knowledge which give power, requires a period of preparation and that it is better so. i.e. We would not permit an ignorant person to be in control of an electrical power house—and for good and obvious reasons—such a person would be a danger to himself and to others. Ancient wisdom, the Secret Knowledge of man and all concerning him, is not just speculative metaphysical hypotheses, but scientific, empirical knowledge!!"

There are secrets as much more powerful than the atom bomb as the atom bomb is more powerful than a firecracker. For that reason the secrets, the eternal truths have been preserved and well guarded down through the ages by certain custodians of the Mysteries. It is now time that this Ancient Wisdom be brought forth into the open for dissemination. *The mysteries will no longer be concealed from anyone who seeks; the great truths will no longer be hidden by dark and concealing parables. Those who will to understand will be clearly given the laws under which man lives and has his being.*

For too long most of us have just accepted what we

are told to believe, accepting too much without investigation. After all, so much conflicting information has been made available, so many half-truths and faulty premises, that it behooves us to study and learn the truth instead of allowing ourselves to be lulled to sleep or to be deceived and inveigled by those who make mysteries and millions and achieve self-gratification out of possibilities borrowed from the truth. Disbelief and criticism and constant denials have kept the facts of interplanetarians from the public, causing confusion and making way for falsifications and imposters, who have misled many. Let desire be our keynote to the finding out of truth.

There are a variety of truth-seekers—those who are just beginning to realize that churchianity is stalemated, and to question cultural traditions and old established dogmas, creeds and theories, and those who are more advanced in their understanding, having stepped aside from the ordinary flow of the mass consciousness* on Earth. Unless a religion is unlimited in intellectual scope and can answer to the needs of the intellect and appeal to the logical mind as well as

---
* Consciousness exists upon three distinct planes: simple consciousness, self-consciousness and Cosmic consciousness. Self-consciousness is the state of perception in which the majority of the people exist today. The human mind has risen out of the lowest type of savagery into the stage of reasoning with the ability to reason from a given point or thought into distinct and, to his limited knowledge, new hypothesis."

the heart, those who need the food of the intellect to satisfy their deep longings will seek it elsewhere.

According to a review of the events of 1956 there are some two hundred and fifty-eight religious bodies in the United States. The four major denominations are Protestant, Roman Catholic, Jewish, and Eastern Orthodox, besides the many minor religious divisions or churches. Each has its appeal to the minds of those in their various stages of manifestation, and we grant that they are inspiring to such of those as understand only so much. All these religious societies have their places in the scheme of things, and their purpose must be fulfilled, although as a whole they leave many blank spaces in man's understanding of himself.

Our Brothers revealed that there are few religious orders on this planet Earth that teach the true teachings of Jesus, the Christ, and the detail of his life. Of those institutes that do, the majority have only incomplete teachings to give. Though our Brothers do not acknowledge our many religious divisions, they do not oppose them. They recognize that all men are 'right' within the limitations of their awareness and beliefs, and that our religions are what they are because of our lack of understanding of our Creator and the purpose of life.

> All present religions [while having many good points] were founded on man's limited interpretation of the will of God, and founded on that inter-

pretation it cannot be perfect for no man is perfect. However, the body of ideas and institutions that make up what we mean when we speak of Christianity did not come out of a historical void. In order to understand our present religions we need to understand the Kabbala*, the most mysterious of all the mystery teachings. It is the essence of all religions and philosophies with the addition of greater and more far reaching wisdom. Its very simplicity has been its concealment, for in simple symbols it conceals the vast truth of the Source of all things. Anyone who understands the Kabbalistic teachings has the key to all ancient religions, myths and legends, for it is the complete record of the Ancient Wisdom.

Our Brothers discreetly advised me, "Think not too deeply of the book you call the Holy Bible. If you do not understand it, you will be baffled and misled. It will be difficult to realize the Truth if you become confused."

---

* The three greatest books of the Kabbala (the bible of ancient antiquity) are The Book of Formation, The Book of Splendor and The Book of Revelation. The Kabbala in its more modern form was compiled by Moses Deleon about 1305 A.D. from manuscripts and traditions of the secret schools.

The mysteries of the original Kabbala were in existence long before Semitic monotheisms—Judaism, Christianity, Islam—before Hebrew magic which came forth from Egyptian, Babylonian, Canaanite and Hellenistic sources. The Kabbalistic teachings existed long before written treatises, or any system was embodied in Hebrew books written from the sixth to the tenth centuries on the Kabbala.

Branches of so-called Kabbalistic work have made up evidence in favor of their theological ideas, and from the most unlikely sources. From these confused systems stemmed the priesthoods, human sacrifice, sorcery, and barbarous, medieval campaigns, as well as perversion.

Perhaps you maintain that every good Christian thinks deeply of the Bible. But let us see what statistics reveal. According to the following classification* of people we find:

	BELIEVE IN BIBLE	DENY BIBLE
Sociologists	14%	86%
Biologists	18%	82%
Psychologists	19%	81%
Historians	32%	68%
Physicists	34%	65%

Though our Christian Bible is based on the most ancient of Hebrew teachings, it is not infallible. Prior to it, all teachings were secret, and hidden in symbolism.

Though a historical document of human behaviorism since man first learned to write, the Bible is full of allegory and parables written in such a manner that one who is not familiar with the Eastern mind cannot understand it; *they take the literal meaning and do not see the symbolism entailed.* We of the Western world think with the Western mind, and the Bible is a record of sayings and doings of the Eastern mind, which is different and works different.

We can also say the Bible is but a key whereby one can unlock the teachings of the Mysteries. Only by knowing the Eastern world symbology and meaning can we arrive at the true meaning of Jesus' teachings. Considering the teachings as given in the churches today it is surprising that people believe as much as they do for we have not the whole Truth; there is so much eliminated and altered in the Bible.

---
*Louis T. Talbot (President of The Bible Institute of Los Angeles), "Can An Intelligent Person Believe the Bible." (1942)

A lot of the most wonderful Biblical writings were set aside by the council of Nicaea as not being necessary for man's salvation. The layman believes in the originality of Christ's doctrine, having no awareness that the doctrine is, in fact, based in large part on sources that have little to do with Judaic tradition, and that they do not even appear in the Bible. Many of the people of the world have accepted illogical teachings because they have always been taught that they must not question the teachings of the Bible. In approaching that Great Mind we call God there is no necessity for using anything but that God-given power called reason.

In thinking that the universe revolves around ourselves few of us realize that during the time of Jesus, the Christ, the multitudes who had neither eyes to see nor ears to hear were in exactly the same state as the people today. Jesus could not give but a part of his great teachings because of the lack of understanding of the great mass of people at that time. He tried to give the mystery teachings to them, but they would not accept them; they were not ready to be given the inner mysteries or essence of Truth about their relationship to God.

Jesus, the Christ, and his immediate followers were unquestionably versed in the Kabbalistic teachings which he taught in two manners, one to the great multitudes and another to the select few who formed the apostles and disciples. We know he said to the disciple Matthew: "Unto you it is given to know the mysteries of the Kingdom of Heaven but unto them it is not given because seeing they see not for their eye is closed and their ear is deaf and they cannot understand."

However, the teachings of Jesus remained pure and unprofaned up to the time of the reign of Constantine, The Great. Henceforth they became desecrated and perverted by the race consciousness of that era which sought darkness rather than the Light. There were those whose concepts distorted the true teachings that the race of people might be kept in place through fear. The people today are still being given the same half-truths that were given then. For this reason it is difficult to give the mysteries to the great mass of people today, for they want things to make them feel good, and to be told only what they want to hear and that which pleases them.

So few there are who know about their own religion, its origin, its fundamental principles, its history, or the symbolism involved. The trouble is there are doctrinal differences among the churches, and our modern Christian religions are for the most part bigoted and confusing, too often incomplete and fanatical, and therefore have resulted in people discarding the faith of the past and substituting it with doubt. If we listen to the inner-self we will be astonished to find that for a long time truth has been knocking on the door of our consciousness, and that the fault has been our comprehension. Rather than to demolish the entire fabric of our present religious beliefs we need to teach a deeper comprehension of the spiritual truths imbedded therein, and to build on these. Knowledge that has brought us to our present understanding need not be cast aside, neither should we limit ourselves from gaining a better understanding by assuming we cannot learn more, or that we have all the truth and there is no more to add and nothing to take away.

To gain a realization of happiness or heaven does not mean we have prepared ourselves for a life of inactivity. Each day we should make real, and be conscious of the happiness we believed hitherto we must die to attain. We cannot shirk responsibility. It is an act of weakness to try to shift our thoughts and acts upon another, even as we have so long blamed hell and the devil. If some one tells you of a way to happiness, and you follow in that belief, you may prove or disprove its personal value, but nevertheless, you must be the final arbiter of your own destiny.

Most of us have heard or used the expression, "If only I knew that this is so. How can I know?"

The average person has not reached an understanding whereby he may reach absolute Knowing. First comes desire and then effort, for no one can gain Knowing by sitting still. It is not enough to say that this is or that is so, only to find it contradicting life as we know it. We, ourselves, are responsible as to whether we will recognize the truth when it is given to us, and that depends on our comprehension. With understanding comes the ability to know. But if we do not understand that life is a manifestation of law, if we don't know ourselves for the truth that we are, we have not approached Truth, we cannot recognize the Truth of another or that of the Universe.

The only way we can find the higher truth which is beyond the limitations of materiality in which we have our being, is by elevating the state of our consciousness to such a degree that we realize, hear, and feel with the inner, higher self, rather than our physical ears and eyes. Our goal must be a balance in all things if we hope to master all things and attain to Knowing.

Since Truth is the highest teacher there is, we must seek that truth as a quality rather than a personality. Truth is positively impersonal and is related in no way to any individual. Those who have studied this or followed that teacher to gain truth usually find only disappointment.

Many persons who have gained a little enlightenment or who may have been seekers for years have been heard to declare, "This is all there is; no one can teach me now, I have found what is truth for me," yet in reality it may be but a smattering of truth. That which may be comprehensible and acceptable to one man as truth, another neither believes to be truth nor understands it. This is because Truth can only be absorbed by each individual in accordance with their capacities for understanding that truth. As children in our public schools are in different grades of education, all peoples are in different grades of understanding in the school of life, few seeing through the same eyes. No matter how high we may attain, we can find greater heights beyond. We must not only make what *understanding* we have active, but *it must have growth*, else we have stagnation and death. In previous wars man has waged he has poured out the life-blood of millions of his kind, having not grown away from the idea that each war fought is 'a war to end all wars,' though none have yet brought lasting peace. If we can say that men have had growth, they have progressed mostly in their ability to destroy their brothers, to slaughter them, giving little or no thought to working together on a never-ceasing task of building a better world. Neither have they grown in the comprehension of the fact that they must face their future and meet the effects from the causes they set up in the present, not only singly as individuals but collectively as a mass of people.

Chapter Four

COSMIC CYCLES

IN 1955 our Brothers imparted to me that our planet Earth was going through a cycle change, that the year nineteen hundred and fifty-five was the ebb of the Old Age before transiting into the seventh cycle or new Earth cycle. Also that critical conditions would come upon the Earth, many disasters effecting all parts of the globe and the people living upon it.

In referring to the teachings of THE BROTHERHOOD OF THE WHITE TEMPLE, INC., we are told:

"When we say Earth Cycle we are referring to certain definite movements of consciousness to and from this Earth to other planets. The beginning and end of such an epoch or age marks the beginning of an Earth cycle or the end of another. Seven of these Earth cycles constitute a Cosmic Cycle, each of which are divided into seven minor divisions.

The reason the first Earth Cycle was called the Golden Age is that at that time man was a perfect channel for the expression of God. At the end of the seventh Earth Cycle he will also be the same thing. The same balance will again be struck. 'As in the beginning so in the end.'

May of the year 1956 marked the long awaited beginning of the New Age or seventh Earth Cycle of material Earth during which the power and the Kingdom of the Christ is to come to man, though first, mankind must pass through a period in which the things of darkness will multiply for a time."

Our Brothers continued, "Some of your people will advance to a more highly evolved planet to incarnate. Many will go to a planet on a lower level of existence, yet on the same level as Earth at the time they leave it. As a planet passes through a cycle change, it is always progressing; the people who have prepared themselves will also advance in universal growth and understanding."

Man is far more ancient on this Earth than we have been taught. There was a time in the far past history of our planet when there were those on higher evolved planets in this and other systems who did not move along with the great mass consciousness, who refused to live in brotherly relationship, who were arrogant and unruly, seeking to hold back man's progress. They were exiled to this Earth, as well as to some other worlds set aside for this purpose, that they might work out their salvation in their own way. These were the 'fallen angels' referred to in our Scriptures.

While civilizations on our Earth have risen and fallen, beings on other planets in this system have steadily continued to progress intellectually, spiritually and socially by fulfilling the will of the Creator. This

Earth has been the planet of slowest evolution and is the only warring planet in this system.

Our present civilization is far from the highest that has ever existed upon this Earth. The most advanced was most certainly that which existed before the fall of Man. Of the several highly advanced civilizations since, the Atlantean epoch undoubtedly attained to the highest culture, although the Chinese are also said to be one of the oldest civilized races, which at one time would have made our present white race seem like barbarians in comparison.

When souls of one civilization had reached their highest peak of development, they passed on to reincarnate on a higher evolved planet of a vibration they had become attuned to. They were superseded by a wave of consciousness, or souls, from a lower evolved planet who were attuned to the vibratory rate of this planet, and who had to begin to climb again the ladder of atonement round by round. A soul has its individual tonal vibration, and like a magnet it is attracted to a frequency of vibration it is in harmony with. As the vibration of our planet Earth increases to a higher frequency evolving towards a spiritual state, souls of a higher consciousness are being attracted to it to reincarnate here.

The ultimate purpose of creation is eternal progression. In this progression of evolution from body to body and planet to planet we pass from grade to grade in the school of life and rise in spiritual elevation to higher states of expression and service. Many times we fail by our own volition and have to repeat the same grade. The progress we've made in previous lives we briefly repeat in each life till we come to the point where we left off, then we begin the toilsome process of acquiring the new. This accounts for the rapid advancement made by some, while others slowly work their way up. There are those on this planet and other low planets in other solar systems whose reality exceeds the mass consciousness, at times even into Illumination.* In a hundred years or so the state of Illumination will be a common heritage, and the great majority of humanity will desire and strive to attain it.

Through the process of reincarnation and transmigration civilization has emerged from a fallen state into our present degree of development, for through our incarnations we have been continually striving, consciously and unconsciously, to become aware of our Oneness with God as we were in the beginning. As to the heights this present civilization may rise and as to the progress our world makes, all men are responsible, even the most lowly. "All that man is, is because of his wisdom; all that he shall become is the result of his Cause." There is no set limit as to what we can do, except as we so limit ourselves and our Creator. We

---

* " Illumination is that state in which one is consciously aware of his Soul, wherein he becomes one with its Light and Wisdom."

should all accept and act upon the statement of Jesus, the Christ, "Greater works than these shall ye do."

We of Earth talk of living the Christ-life, but that is all. To live the Christ-life means having a working knowledge of those operative laws as taught by Jesus. Mankind has had all of two thousand years to seek, to learn, to try to understand, to actually live the Christ-life, but they have chosen to remain laggards, allowing Cosmic Progression to outdistance them. Men refused Jesus then because they were not sufficiently tempered to understand him, and if he descended to Earth today he would not only be rejected, he would not recognize his teachings as given by our churches called Christian. Since his teachings are so simple and clear, he certainly would wonder how they could have become so changed, corrupted and misunderstood. However, there are ministers and religious teachers who today have arrived at a much broader outlook on life, the body, mind, Spirit, and Soul, and are better able to uplift themselves and humanity. The time has come when many are weary of strife and war, of stress and turmoil. Thousands of people are maturing rapidly, and in their search for truth and greater understanding are receiving it in a different light, with receptive minds and hearts. More shall be ready to accept the coming World Teacher and his message than were ready to accept Jesus.

It is estimated that there are three times as many

people who believe in reincarnation as there are in orthodox Christian faiths. To believe in reincarnation requires no other supposition than that fundamentally accepted by the Christian sects, immortality of soul.* Reincarnation, when properly understood, shows us that God is a just God; it explains every fact and factor in the Bible, and explains everything in life. Jesus gave his disciples exactly the same teaching of reincarnation as was taught in the esoteric schools in the inner circles of the East. "His every act was a portrayal of the life of man, incarnation after incarnation, until he overcomes every experience of life."

Our Brothers reminded me that many people of the planet Earth believe that each soul is created newly for each new body and has never existed elsewhere on the material plane, that we should understand that the soul realizes reincarnation but that the consciousness of man manifesting on the physical plane is veiled by materiality and therefore unaware of former existences, or life in other 'temples.'

> Those who do not accept reincarnation as a reality are those who believe that as God ordains or wills everything is, has been and will be, and they never entertain the thought that the will of God may be functioning according to Infinite Order and subject to Cosmic Law, and that God might be existing *because* of an Infinite Activity, and Infinite Progression. Many find it difficult to accept reincarnation

---
* See reference by Solomon to immortality of the soul: Proverbs 8:22-35

as a reality because, from earliest infancy, they have been taught the soul is created newly and uniquely for each physical body, never having existed on the physical plane previously, and never to enter another physical body in the future, excepting that their present body will be reassembled at some future day of judgment. But where does the soul go between the time of death and the time of resurrection? How can it go to a heaven or a place of punishment if it has not yet been judged? We are not told, because Jesus never taught such a thing, therefore it cannot be found in the New Testament.

There are certain sects who, in studying the Bible, have found certain passages which they take to mean that the soul is a created thing and only becomes immortal when it is saved, as they say, 'Saved by the blood of Jesus,' that it puts off corruption and takes up incorruption. They are so interpreted because they are not read in the light of understanding of Kabbalistic symbolism which tells us very clearly that if the soul is of God and from God then it cannot be separated from the quality of God, that it must have inherent and potential within it all the qualities of its creator, and that the quality of God is one of immortality and continuity of existence. Therefore, the soul has an immortality of existence, but it has in its material manifestation an apparent termination of the immortality because of its loss of consciousness as it passes from life to life, from incarnation to incarnation. That immortal life is realized when one puts aside all the transitory experiences and realizes the true nature of self which always was and is, immortal, but because of the creative power of God in it, man assumes mortality and binds himself into a condition of non-knowing or non-awareness of the Divine Self which is the real and true nature.

The modern Christian religion teaches of the existence of a soul and yet is able to give *no definite proof* that such a thing exists. This is because they do not have the *knowledge* of the mysteries taught by Jesus. He taught the disciples the actual operative knowledge of the laws of God, and taught the people in a different manner. There are only a few of the things he taught recorded in the New Testament. It is a very sketchy manuscript. The fact that Jesus taught reincarnation has been glossed over and veiled until there are few who know it is plainly taught in the four Gospels . The various religious beliefs of our present time and the contradictions we find in them can only be explained by the true teaching of Reincarnation.

There are those of you who may ask, "Is Jesus, the Christ,* known on other planets?" Suffice it to say that a complete record has been kept and preserved of the history of this entire world from the time of its beginning, from the time it evolved to the point where it supported animal life and life known as man, of all the races that have ever lived, and on through the ages to the present time. Jesus has appeared in different parts of the world, and on different worlds constantly since

---

* "Many people confuse the name Jesus with the term Christ. Jesus, was Jesus, the Christ. The word, Christ meant the illumined, the illumined state of consciousness, and the second coming of Christ to you is not the coming of the man, or son, Jesus; it is the coming of the Christ Consciousness to you yourself so you realize the Divine Existence in you."

he appeared as Jesus. All great souls that always labor to bring about Divine At-onement of the universe do not appear in incarnation just once and then quit. *That power which we call Christ is manifest upon all worlds throughout the Cosmos.* It is known by many and varied names, yet it is the one and the same power.

Yes, the New Age, a new dawn of men, has begun and ere it closes the law of incarnation will dissolve. In the beginning, in the Golden Age, man did not taste of death, so in the end before the Cosmic Cycle is completed, man will no longer partake of death in the old accepted sense of the word. The soul will have overcome its bondage to the flesh, which does not mean we die. The physical body will have become a body spiritual, for evolution is tending toward a complete spiritualization of matter. All negative and impure thoughts will be left behind, all disorder washed away, and the lower nature changed and transmuted.

Our Brothers explained, "Everyone possesses what is called a soul, but very few of your people know anything about it or its nature. They should know the soul from the start. A being is born—as a child grows, the soul will need to learn, to be corrected when it branches off the Lighted Path. The spiritual soul of man is like a solar system. Each soul unit, an extension of the Cosmic Soul, is a directing energy that manifests through a 'sun' and twelve centers in the crown of man, activating the physical being, just as all forces and energies are manifested through the sun, activating the twelve planets in their respective positions in the solar system. The material body of man has thirty-three centers in which he should be able to function mentally. When man is balanced in these material centers he is capable of functioning consciously on higher planes of manifestation. Through the consciousness of man the frequency of a planet's vibration is amplified to a higher spiritual state. Man is the channel through which the power of Divine Intelligence manifests. Learn the laws of nature, the true nature of the Soul, and the ways of the Creator."

The thirty-three centers spoken of also refer to the thirty-three principles of the Kabballa. The thirty-three degrees of Masonry stem from these thirty-three principles.

> "Much use is made of Kabbalistic symbolism in the higher degrees of Masonry and even entire rites have been built upon it. The Mason symbolizes the Spiritual plane as the broken triangle, a symbol that he has climbed the seven steps ('the seven ways to bliss' or seven attributes) and passed into the thirty-two degrees and entered the thirty-third which is a symbol of the Supreme plane of the Spirit."

Continuing with the Brotherhood of the White Temple teachings we find as regards the soul:

> "The soul of man that we hear and know so little about, is the actual, directing, activating force in every man's life from a few weeks after birth until the time of transition. That activating principle,

carrying within it the experience and knowledge of the Ages, directs the physical manifestation of man into certain paths of life and certain environments according to the Law of Cause and Effect.

We also know little concerning the relationship of the soul to the Oversoul* or Divine Essence, and the powers that lie inherent and potential in that soul. It is that intangible something which man calls 'the soul' that produces the ego or personality of the individual.

God created man and breathed the breath of life into him. The real and true life of man is the breath of God or Soul of God within him, expressing itself through his physical manifestation. *This soul is the same in all men*, and all souls are 'a part' of the Oneness of God. The soul is also the formless nature of God. It may never be destroyed, but exists eternally. And all things, material or manifest are a result of the concentrated thought of the soul working through the material.

The Ancient Wisdom says the soul has an actual point of manifestation in the physical body. By its very nature it must always manifest and remain in the spiritual plane of consciousness, but also it must manifest through the medium of the fleshly envelope we call the human body. The soul, spiritual in na-

---

* "The Oversoul is the higher, Spiritual quality of man. This term is used because like a mighty bird whose wings spread over the world, the Oversoul broods over the finite expression or body of man and no matter what he does or where he goes, it is always present with its over-shadowing wings.

"The Oversoul never directs man in the wrong channels of life. It is man's own willfulness, it is his manifestation within the negative expression of the world that causes him to go in directions opposite from that of the still small voice or oversoul speaking within him. Man looks only to the outer or external self."

ture, derives that spiritual nature from the source of all being which is God, the Divine Mind, or Universal Consciousness. The quality remains the same regardless of the term by which we designate it.

The ancients taught that the soul is a Spiritual thing, it is not in the physical body, that the physical body is only a vehicle of expression: that it is a vessel into which the Spirit manifests to activate or express in the material world. It perhaps is the bottle into which the wine of the new Spirit is poured and the old bottle must be transmuted and made new. It must become the perfect vessel for the Divine Spirit to manifest in.

In some persons this soul or force is able to flow more freely than in others and they are said to be highly developed spiritually. In everyone the soul expresses itself to some degree through what we call hunches or intuition. However, the average person is not in tune with the Infinite; the objective mind is not trained to recognize the meanings in a true sense. We must change and raise our vibration so that we are perfect instruments through which the soul can operate and express itself freely, for the soul knows all things, and being a part of all things is never wrong. When man has reached this point he is capable of obeying implicitly the direction of the Cosmic Mind — he has regained his heritage, Oneness with the Creator.

Many people think there are new and old souls. There are no such things. All souls have existed in the world since the beginning. The difference is that some souls have worked to master and overcome life to a greater degree than others, as reflected in their life and actions, and we call them old souls; while others just laze along, incarnation after incarnation, doing nothing, and we call them young souls, or lazy souls. We should all get active, and not be lazy. Being accustomed to work in certain grooves, the mind has to be trained into new grooves of thinking and action. Nothing worthwhile is gained by laziness.

Our Brothers assured me that "all of the people of your planet will have to learn to live in a different Light. There are many things that they do and they call it 'sin.' It could be done in a different Light; it would not be a sin."

"Well, what is sin? What is sin to one may not be sin to another. Each and every race of people have had their own peculiar sins or things which they considered sins. However, the only sin a person can make is when a person attempts to break some Divine or Cosmic Law. *The true sin is where one has put themselves out of harmony with Divine Law and lives in darkness.* Keeping the Divine Law is placing ourselves in harmony with the Divine Will. 'Let Thy will, not mine, be done.'

The church teaches that the sins of the father are visited upon the children even unto the third generation, and then they say that God is a just God. The truth is that the condition into which a soul is born is not the result of the sins of the father, but of its own sins committed in past incarnations or lives. We do not suffer from what some one else did, but for what we, ourselves, did in the past. Everything which comes to us comes because of our own actions. God created law, and we either move and live in harmony with that law, or we break ourselves against it—we cannot break the Law.

A misunderstanding of the sacred teachings has caused all man's lack of knowledge of the true nature of himself and of the soul, and it is certain that man, even in spite of all the theologies, is going to emerge into a knowledge of his own soul-self and his own soul-power.

The human soul is like a seed from which springs a plant, on which is a bud, and the bud blossoms into a flower. The flower did not spring at once from the seed. Realize that you will gain from the universe or divine, exactly what you put into it. Do not say, 'I am God's perfect child, open the door and let me come in.' *The door will open when you accomplish by living the life within.* You must realize there is no royal road, only one of growth.

Chapter Five

INTO COSMIC LIGHT

Our Brothers professed that the Creator, in His Infinite Wisdom, condemns not any part of His Creation. Yet people of Earth make a sad mistake; they are the ones who judge others. With greater understanding they would cease to judge. They would only analyze others, and not condemn them for their shortcomings, for each and everyone is learning his lessons in the school of life through experiences and mistakes. Everyone should learn to live in the ever-present, not yesterday or tomorrow. They have only today. The past does not matter except to correct the mistakes made, and remedy the now, so that they will not be repeated. Live from there and the future will always be. I wish to emphasize their statement, "We do not find fault to degrade the people of your planet, but all are reverenced for the Divine Life within. Nor, in His great wisdom, is it the Creator's wishes to cause harm. We must speak Truth. Through understanding and compassion peace will come to your world."

Did you ever perceive that in judging another, you

might be judging yourself? Jesus said, "I judge no man." If he did not judge, who are we that we do so? We should forgive and forget the wrongdoings of another, and look to find their good qualities. By so doing we not only uplift the weaker ones, but ourselves and the whole Cosmos.

The cumulation of all the negative causes which man has set up in the past must be met at the close of every age. The slate must be wiped clean as we enter the new cycle, and we are finding it difficult to meet the rapid inflow of changes from these effects we have created. Change is the trend of the times, and the keynote is a knowledge of the Christ within.

The disheartening thing is as our Brothers concede, "As time goes on the people of the planet Earth do little to help themselves or their conditions. There is no excuse for them to be in the condition they are at this time. If they would seek the Truth they could find it. But in their indifference they haven't time to search for Truth." If they were not so self-centered and foolish they would have done something long ago about the things going on in the world. They should be taking delight in fulfilling the duties of reciprocal love and brotherhood instead of being so completely busy enjoying the misfortunes of their brothers.

The average American is utterly unconcerned as long as he can have a TV set and a new automobile! There are too many people in the world who live only for the moment, accepting things that are placed before them, not attempting to find the way of anything, and allowing themselves to be led continually into destruction by those not caring by what means they attain their power. Men fear enslavement, being blindly unaware that they are already enslaved. They are just drifting along the stream of life instead of charting a course, content to live as they are when there is much room for improvement, for everyone has it in him to become far more than he is. They must be shaken from their outlook and made to realize that in tomorrow the purpose of their existence today will be fulfilled. The proud head of man who has conquered most everything *but himself*, must be bowed and he must again learn to turn to the Creator to lead him in the ways of Light, Truth and Righteousness. Man has yet to learn the great lesson of brotherly state and the love of the Creator who put them here.

Man has dared trifle with God's Laws and His Creation rather than fulfill his purpose in service, working with Him as One. If man had learned the laws of the Creator and lived in harmony with them he would have been so rewarded and justice would now reign throughout our land. Instead man will now need to be strong enough to meet the consequences of his own thoughts and actions since the things he has done will be returned unto him a hundred-fold. He will need to 'lift himself up by his bootstraps,' up out of the chaotic river of humanity, to stand upon the bank and observe the masses in their true state of existence as they go drifting by, struggling forms, struggling nations, becoming more submerged as they wallow along in the murky darkness of Illusion. He must learn to meet the effects of causes in such a way that he will set up protective causes rather than destructive ones. If he will sit at God's feet he must have an unprejudiced mind, he must realize that the things which are happening are not in the nature of punishment, but something for him to face calmly, without fear, without anger, meeting each experience as one of life's lessons, as something to be gained. He will then learn to live an impersonal life in the present, in accordance with Divine Principle and Divine Love. There will be no need to fear the future, as the things which might enter his life to harm him will merely pass away. God's Presence watches over, and His Power protects the one who loves rather than hates. It is that man should be willing to look for good in all life, in every experience, and to 'keep his soul alive to truth whereever found.'

Our Brothers informed me that our leaders on Earth *have not* taught the laws of the Creator and of Nature as they apply to our planet, nor do our various religions admit the possibility of man on other planets lest they be proven wrong. They, the leaders, think of their world as being the only inhabited place, choosing to believe they are the only ones who live. There are many worlds that exist. There are ancient records on our planet that tell it is only one of many civilized worlds. There are a vast number that are evolved far beyond ours. Our greatest knowledge is that of young children in comparison with the masters of science in the Cosmic university. When the Creator manifested the galaxies He also manifested certain Law by which the solar system must operate. There are thirty-three fixed laws a planet must be governed by in order to be actually and perfectly balanced in nature. Nature in itself is the thirty-three laws. Each world should know these laws and abide by them so they may have harmony and true love to keep them in balance.

When we say 'nature' an ordinary responsive thought is, 'Oh, nature--the birds and bees, flowers and trees, the sunshine, winds and the seven seas.' But man must go deeper into nature to understand her, to understand himself. He should seek to regain the knowledge and simplicity of nature and her secrets that were once his, for nature is the schoolhouse provided for him in which to learn. Down through the ages nature's rebel son has grown away from her, and selfishly and aggressively tries to dominate the world upon which he dwells, tries to improve upon nature instead of living naturally and closer to her. Although many have attempted to study and understand nature, only a few have succeeded in finding the path which leads to the understanding of Cosmic Law.

The only permanent things are change and principle. Principle does not change, but everything in nature is continually changing, every moment, every second; and that change is rhythmic, following given cycles. Nothing happens by accident; everything in this world is planned according to unchanging Principle for nature does not theorize; she is truth personified. All the great empires of antiquity fell because they stood still; they refused to change, to grow and advance. Every being has a great capacity for change, but since man is slave to his egotism, most of us dislike change, especially when it is going to interfere with our mean pride and some of our selfish and more negative ways, and so we resist it, like a balking mule. But wise is he who tries to live conformably to the nature of all things of which he is one.

Our Brothers explained that when one is told to study nature, it is meant that he is to study her in all her phases, animate and inanimate; that it is essential that he study the material and spiritual nature of the physical body as well as the material and spiritual consciousness, and temporal conditions around him. Nature is forever one, as a whole, but infinite in expression. Her great natural forces are invisible to our eyes, and even to our most subtle senses. There is no greater force in nature than that of the human soul, ego, or consciousness.

It is deemed wise to make nature and all her manifestations our field of study.

However, the average student rambles through many clumsy experiments and clutters his mind up with warring and clashing ideas. He must first understand that all things in the world are dual. For anything to exist it must have two polarities; for anything to be balanced it must have two focal points with an equal distribution of weight or quality.

The Infinite and the Finite are two very important polarities. The Infinite may be considered as the All, whereas the finite may be looked upon as a particular part of the All. The finite moves because of the movement of the Infinite. Everything that exists on the finite plane has form and being solely because of its extension from the Infinite. The finite mind cannot see the Infinite, but it can sense its existence and learn many things which move near Infinity in Time and Space.

Always equally in the most infinitesimal as well as the greatest part of nature there is all pervading Light; it is in All Things. This Immortal Light is indestructible, but ever changing and always remaining in an order within itself, regardless of how divided.

As we grow into Cosmic Comprehension, broadening our knowledge of nature, we shall find that those phases of nature that are now hidden from our understanding will come into our range of vision.

For those who desire to master the conditions of life, the first law of nature is maintaining a physical, mental and spiritual condition of balance, including emotional balance. There is a constant nervous, mental and physical strain impressed on every person, making living in this world today a difficult thing. There is a constant upheaval in the life of man because of the continual clash between the order of order and the order of disorder. All the world seems to be drifting into a state of emotional unrest as we find ourselves swayed this way and that by propaganda, emotionalism or our own desires and forces. At the same time there is an unrest among the people as we are in the process of changing from an old order into a new one. Although we have already entered a New Age, we are still clinging to the old and have not grasped the new. As a result, everything seems topsy-turvy as we sway back and forth in our uncertainty of leaving the old and accepting that which is new. Nevertheless, "All is moving to higher and greater purposes, always creating, always testing, and always enlarging. A living something, completion within completions, polarity within polarities, order within orderings. All moving through Time and Space toward the Greater Becoming."

It was quite a revelation when our Brothers explained that the vibration of the Earth's orbit is changing rapidly into a higher frequency, but the people are so misbehaved the planet is out of balance. It is unbalanced with disorder and chaos. The unbalanced condition causes a vacillating motion which impels the Earth off its course. The vibration of our planet is in conflict with the vibration of its orbit for it is not increasing in a corresponding high rate of vibration due to the low thought frequency of the mass consciousness upon it. You would not think that it would be possible for your automobile to run if the gears on it were running one on one speed and one on another, would you? The mass as a whole could, if they would, prevent much trouble, as a planet functions under a frequency which is established only by the inhabitants who dwell upon it. They could change the course of events and even prevent the last phase of Armageddon. Nevertheless, if the people do not increase their vibration to the point that the frequency of the Earth will harmonize with that of the orbit, they will experience freakish and serious accidents and deaths. Our daily news reports are confirmation of this forewarning. Our Brothers also foresee that there will come a time when people of Earth will grasp at almost any belief, or help from any source, if they think it will protect them from trouble, despair and destruction, for by the very force of destruction around them they will be driven into a greater and stronger seeking for the Creator, until finally they see there is nowhere to turn except to the Divine within themselves.

Since the Fall of Man, that entering of negation, the movement in the Cosmos has not been as ordered as it could be as man has been greatly affected by that influx of negation. Man's existence is for the purpose of gathering experience, each experience completed bringing more knowledge and power to the Cosmos as a whole. It is that man's purpose in life has been to transmute disorder into order, but this he has failed to do. Man fails himself, God, and the entire universe, when he fails to overcome the negative in his own life. He has long forgotten that when, in the beginning, he was given dominion over this Earth and all thereon, that he was to rule by Love and Love alone. Just "one single moment of perfect Divine Love can bring us eternal freedom from the bondage that effects the great mass of mankind."

Only through Divine Love can order and harmony be brought forth. Since through the Wisdom and Great Divine Love of the Creator, disorder is transmuted into order, the time has now arrived when the disordered movement must become ordered despite man's failure to do his part, and the adjustment will be severe for him, for he has not prepared himself. He has not been about his Father's business! The fact that he has remained in darkness, handicapped by his worst fault, hypocrisy and selfishness—low vile greed, lust for his own satisfaction at the expense of the world—can only result in a reaction similar to a monkey-wrench tossed into the cogs of a great machine. Not man-made law but Cosmic Principle prevails!

Science has discovered that there is such a thing as magnetic currents that flow through all matter. They are not speaking of the magnetic polarities. The Ancient Atlanteans had the knowledge of that magnetic power and they knew that that magnetic flow which cannot be detected by the same way that the magnetic pole may be, that is main flow of static energy, but that that magnetic flow flows through the entire Earth, forming as it were, a web just like a steel framework of a large building. If you break that framework somewhere it becomes weakened and there may be a collapse. The magnetic flow flowing through the central nucleus of all matter forms definite channels, rivers and streams that criss-cross each other and that helps to maintain matter and substance in a more or less static condition, but if anything happens to disturb that flow there is a collapse, not only of that magnetic current but of that web itself and it causes upheavals.

Every vibration when born of thought and emotion (action) produces a reaction in the universe that is immeasurable, and the Ancients knew that the thoughts of man have a tremendous effect upon that magnetic current; that is, that they attract it or repel it, and they knew that tremendous negative and fearful thoughts had repulsive power upon those magnetic currents.

Thoughts constantly emitted from all individuals form an ocean or river of thoughts which completely surrounds the earth to a distance of approximately 1500 feet. That follows the contour of the land. It flows up mountains, down valleys, and across the ocean. Man thinks and has his being in the bottom of the 1500-foot deep ocean of thoughts. Even though many of us think only thoughts of peace and are constantly breaking down negative thoughts, still there is at times a gradual increase of disordered thought.

With the conditions of hate, greed, fear and error prevalent in our world, there is unquestionably a tremendous weakening of the magnetic web. The magnetic stresses and strains such conditions are creating can bring collapse and great catastrophes. Nevertheless everyone of you who steps upon the Path of Light to follow the Christ instead of man, will be of assistance in bringing the final balance about with much less tragedy, for the more ordered the movement becomes the more order and harmony will be established among the races of mankind, and therefore an easing of the stress upon the magnetic lines of force. The strength of the universe depends upon you and the part you play, however small and humble, in the eternal scheme of things. There must be spiritual as well as material preparation. "There must be channels and gateways open so there will be a perfect balance of power that has to come about so the Earth can resume its normal orbit in relationship to the whole."

Perhaps man will step out into the Cosmic Light and fulfill his purpose when he fully realizes that his existence is a fulfillment of the purpose of the Infinite One. Though man is a tiny atom in the great reaches of Infinity, yet without him nothing would have existed as a material creation, for through him the forces of Infinity, the intangible part of the Cosmic power manifests, though as yet only immaterial radiations from the immaterial are measurable by man. Surely, man should be proud of his place in the Cosmic scheme!

Chapter Six

CAUSE AND EFFECT

We must face reality—the realty of what is happening. Man is in the condition in which he is today in the world because he is out of harmony with Divine Law. The turmoils of today have been bred by man through avarice, selfishness, prejudice, malice, distrust and aggression. Man has in the past set up certain causes which he must now meet as effects, for that is the law—the Law of Causes and Effect* which no man ever made, yet under which every man lives and has his being whether he cares to admit it or not. It has been commonly referred to as "whatsoever a man soweth, that shall he also reap." Those causes have cumulated into effects we are now confronted with, and because the causes were so often negative and evil, man faces certain perils brought forth in those effects.

It is vitally important to man's welfare and future that he realize he faces the results of his erring ways

---

* There is one great law of compensation—the Law of Cause and Effect, and this law directs our destiny. It is an infinite law and no finite creature can break it by the smallest or greatest action. It is embodied in everything, material or immaterial and everything exists in form because this law exists."

which are creeping upon him from all sides. It is not necessary to recount the many incidents of the wrath of nature, freakish, unexplainable accidents, sickness and disease, for the observant person knows they have been occurring. To enumerate further, he faces the loosening of evil forces upon the Earth; he faces the results of creating hazard in loosening radio-active fallout into Earth's atmosphere; he faces the results of his man-made law of competition—a law of death. He faces the effects of the cruelty of vivisection; the medical tyranny and Drug Trusts. He is confronted with the lack of a truly 'free' and virile press which could expose the danger we are in, and help bring about a genuine peace. He has witnessed promotion of racialism and decisions made on non-segregation, a problem to be solved by peaceful, voluntary efforts, and not by force. He faces what will come of working the first four months of every year for the tax collector. He is facing the pitfalls of a nation on the 'installment plan' with a trillion dollar debt, and mortgages on all our futures. Then there are the results of 'hidden hunger' brought on by consumption of chemically raised foods on depleted soil. Also he will pay the price of a drastically inadequate educational system. Last, yet perhaps first of all, he faces the power of a subversive faction determined to keep truth from mankind. This group consists of really powerful individuals, who, for selfish purposes only, really run the world's governments, and who dare not let it be known that there is even greater power than theirs. The leaders of our various nations are but 'fronts' and tools, but such a condition cannot continue for long as there are those in our governments who will try with all their power to guide the world into a state of peace and brotherhood.

Then in the final phase man must face the changing of the poles of this Earth—a natural occurrence which is met on other planets without the loss of life, but for this planet Earth, the presumption is that half its population will be wiped away in one great housecleaning event because the mass consciousness has failed to keep pace with the cyclic progress ordained for its own life-force. Our Brothers of sister planets have laid the ground-work and set into motion specific plans which are being carried out in preparation for the time of the shift. Survival will depend largely on how receptive man will be to the timely warnings when given by our Brothers and the few of our scientists who are receiving help from them.

In this world of ours we have everything necessary for a beautiful existence, and there is no need for lack or inflation. Every person could have a life of Utopia —but what can the matter be? There isn't anything wrong with the world; it's the people that inhabit it. A heaven would not be heaven if it were not for the condition of things that occupy it. A hell would not be bad if it were not for the people that make it so. Although man dwells on one of the most fertile planets in the Universe, and although he was endowed with the God-given power to make of life and the world a paradise, he is continually engaged in strife and war, and makes but futile efforts in the right direction.

Man himself creates every condition on Earth; he alone creates the good or the bad which comes to him during the course of his life—his consciousness is at the bottom of his troubles. He cannot rightly lay the blame elsewhere. With all these realities man is facing it can be seen that people have ceased to understand each other and are failing to cooperate in their undertakings. If the people of the world did understand each other today would there be the conditions existent that are existent? Man could, if he willed, change all that completely. He can and should make this divided world an undivided one—the multiple superficial boundaries and false divisions must be dissolved. Since the present is changing, he cannot live as he did before, satisfying personal aspirations and practicing destruction. He will have to reform in his ways and thinking. It is absolutely true that if man cannot find or make a heaven here on Earth in his everyday life, he will never find it anywhere else, though he search unto the end of eternity.

Our Brothers are aware that cultural traditions and the beliefs of our forefathers to which we have clung, have not promoted spiritual growth in man; they have done a great deal to lower him spiritually, to retard his unfoldment. As they have implied, if man would change his ways, learn to know himself, to know Nature, and apply that knowledge with wisdom, the last great battle of Armageddon would be averted. But sadly enough, it is later than you think; there is little time left for a definite change to be made in the mass consciousness—for a change to be made in man's attitude towards life, in his mind and in his heart. Yet there is hope, for man is sole arbiter of his destiny, though currently he moves forward through the wanton destruction of the present order of things, reaping a harvest of 'weeds and thorns', suffering, disease, ignorance and waste, the results of his wrong thoughts and actions. But, at last, the old will go, and there will emerge a new and better world, and an original harmony of movement, and an orderly universe.

The Earth and all planets in the galaxy have been slightly off balance, but a change has begun which will gradually bring all into balance. When the change reaches a certain point, the position of the Earth's axis will shift, changing the present location of the north and south poles. There will be tremendous earthquakes, parts of the globe sinking and rising. When land masses disappear beneath the waters, others reappear that the equilibrium of the planet be maintained. Following this there will be dimensional changes and man will gain a new concept of God's creation. The relationship of one planet to another will change so there will be *free movement* of material beings and of souls from lower evolved worlds to higher evolved worlds as well as vice versa. However, there are many things that have to occur first that are only now beginning, such as manifestation of power and force man has never dreamed of!

Therefore it is urgent that man prepare himself to fit in the New Age we have already entered—*a New Age that is not of Earth alone but is a Cosmic thing manifesting upon all planets of all systems*. The Universe will reach a balance, but so must man who so long has been off balance, more materially inclined than spiritually inclined. He is a threefold being and must become mentally, physically and spiritually balanced or there will be no place for him in the New Age. He will need to attain a spiritual attitude towards life in which fear, rankling hatred and the spirit of revenge is eliminated and replaced with Divine Love. He must become aware of the power he has unknowingly used and so carelessly exercised every moment of his life.

As highly evolved as our Brothers are, they admit that they yet have much to learn from the Creator, for the path never ends. If a man climbs to the mounain peak before him, he finds before his vision magnificent vistas of loftier peaks to attain. As he comes into fuller expression of the Cosmic, he perceives new and grander roads to greatness. However, our Brothers have interrupted their advancement to a degree in order to do their part to safeguard this planet Earth from destruction. Anything drastic happening to one planet would affect all because of their relation to one another. Nevertheless, they do not interfere with Nature; she will have her way. There will be many changes in our weather, and conditions will be unpleasant. (This can be summarized in the unusual winds, tornadoes, floods, volcanic eruptions, fires, earthquakes, storms, sea and air disasters). Weather, astronomical and scientific forecasts will prove inaccurate in many instances.

Our Brothers disclosed that they are busy trying to keep our planet in balance, for the destructive experiments made in nuclear research by the different governments affect the already off-balanced condition of the Earth. These various governments of our world are not of any assistance, whatever; they are doing many things that are destructive. Our Brothers went on to say that they work only in harmony with the laws of the Creator; they would not take measures to arrest the governments in their destructiveness by the only means they could understand (war and aggression), but that they were taking steps to warn them to do the Creator's Will, which would be very difficult for them to comprehend; that they would hold a conference soon. The Guardians, our Brothers, do not exhibit their powers or intervene except under stress of absolute necessity.

Because material science is stripped of social and spiritual science, because their efforts are made from effect to effect whereas they could achieve greater success if they worked from cause to effect, our scientists do not know how to take care of what they create, such as radiation fallout. As more and more radioactivity gathers high in our upper atmosphere, the danger lies in decomposition of all living matter. Of the green 'fire-balls' that have been observed throughout the world, one type, sent down from gigantic space-laboratories, has been used to neutralize and absorb concentrations of radiation created through our bomb experiments, otherwise radiation would be more prevalent in our atmosphere than it is. More recently scientists of our neighboring planets have widely replaced the use of the 'fire-ball' with another force, manifested as a high frequency ray.

As early as April 1954 our Brothers told me that my government had accidentally created a dangerous by-product in producing the cobalt bomb that was far worse than any H-bomb. "If they discover what they have they will play with it like a cat with a mouse; if they do not discover it, it is possible they may make a disastrous slip. A slight change of a few degrees temperature would be fatal!" I understand that this by-product had to be nullified through a higher power.

Later I was told that the atmosphere of our planet was in bad condition. That it would cause destruction and severe sickness for the people. And they hoped our government would become cognizant of what it had done before they went too much farther with their experiments. In January 1956 they referred again to the government: "If your government would lay aside their experiments in nuclear fission and study the change in Nature's conditions, they would be of recourse to their people. The government should refrain from the series of tests they have planned. One in particular is very dangerous. In the process of detonation their expected conversion results and amounts of energy release will produce effects quite different from anything they have knowledge of. It may not cause destruction at once, but it would not be long. It will change your planet's atmospheric condition. *Their experiments have already caused much trouble they know nothing about.* There are many things to happen which your people cannot control."

Here they were foretelling of the tests made at the Pacific proving ground and particularly referring to Cherokee, the second test detonation in Operation Redwing, whose demoniacal fury was released into the heavens on May the twenty-first, 1956. This test, so it was said, was delayed ten days in a series of postponements because of climatic conditions. Nevertheless it was rumored that it was not under perfect control and did not prove successful as expected. Except for flowery description little was reported at first, then two top TV commentators stated the bomb was seven miles off its target; that the mighty shock wave hit a nearby island where there were technical recording instruments, which were destroyed. Also the power of the blast was so gargantuan that it ripped the air with terrific pressure and heat waves over thousands of square miles; that the incandescent intensity of light penetrated and blanched shadow and substance to the degree that the bodies of the task group appeared much as when you view one's shadowy anatomy through the fluoroscope. Following this TV report, newspaper reports made contradiction, stating that the bomb was two and/or three miles off target. Those of you who diligently follow the news on these research experiments and rocket shoots know that the majority do not prove successful as planned and anticipated, being but impractical and costly.

We cannot forget the ghastly A-bomb dropped over Hiroshima in '45 as merely a passing horror. Neither can we set aside as something to be forgotten, and considered only as a means of protection in event of warfare, the n u c l e a r tests made thereafter. All, however great or however small, will reverberate somewhere in our world. We've scattered seed and shall reap the harvest. When a thermonuclear test is made there may not be an immediate manifestation as a result, but it sets up a current of energy in the ether of space within the strata of our atmosphere which returns again to us in a like condition though more concentrated. Consider the so-called sonic blasts we are told are caused by jet planes or supersonic fighter planes, breaking the sound barrier. Often there is no plane in the area at the time of the concussion. On such occasions, what then is the answer? 'Echoes' of A-and-H-bomb detonations? We may well experience more severe effects as we continue to release deadly chemical elements into our atmosphere. It is even possible that our planet itself may be effected to the extent that it will be rent apart.

In the June twenty-fifth, 1956 issue of the Newsweek Magazine it is stated that "on one great point or issue —fallout radiation—opinions have always been sharply divided." This article admits in part the serious effects of radiation, however denying any evidence that it effects weather or climate. To quote in part: "Last week in Washington the National Academy of Science published the first explicit and definite fallout report. The academy has spent a year evaluating the results of countless animal experiments and reports on human victims, including the survivors of Hiroshima and Nagasaki, Marshall Islanders and Japanese fishermen. Its concensus confirmed what some scientists have long warned: *Even the lowest levels of radiation can have serious effects.*"

"The academy supported the AEC's claim that nuclear tests do not raise the earth's level of rays to a dangerous degree; but it verified that any atomic war would instantly change the global radiation picture for the worse, leaving mankind more susceptible to leukemia, c a n c e r s, eye cataracts, sterility and shortening of life."

Yet in the May fourteenth number of Newsweek, an article appears which reeks of mean pride in destruction at the expense of the nation. To quote in part: "The U. S. at last is capable of dropping an H-bomb—the equivalent of 10 million tons of TNT—from an airplane at 50,000 feet. To prove it, the U.S. is conducting Operation Redwing—a series of thermonuclear tests off Eniwetok Atoll in the Pacific."

This is followed by a statement that is in contradiction to the June twenty-fifth article, quote: "The radio-active fallout is of little danger to the world or even to those within the vicinity of the explosion; as it contributes to the radio-active background against which we all live, it is even less important."

To quote the article of June twenty-fifth: "The most startling revelation was not about present dangers but the perils of mutations in future generations." It would seem contradiction is an excellent instrument to keep the mass of people confused as to what is true or false, and drifting in a rudderless boat in a sea of befuddled thoughts.

To continue quote of May fourteenth magazine to exemplify costly expenditures involved, "The first explosion was part of a vast atom-and-hydrogen-bomb test which will cost more than $150 million [attention Mr. Taxpayer] exclusive of service equipment and nuclear material, and requires 13,500 men, 118 aircraft, 31 boats and 22 ships."

Our current attempt to acquire greater power through the atom, and our handling of the problem of space flight is maladjusted as well as a waste of our resources. Energies intended for man's welfare, the forces our leaders and proponents of nuclear fission have employed to create destruction, are the same forces that can be used to create constructively. It would be far wiser to take time to marshal these powers constructively rather than destructively, and to make more effort to achieve and finance a world-wide peace movement which is far more urgent, and vitally essential if man expects to survive on this old Earth. We should never forget that nature has plenty of worlds to experiment with—man only has one!

Chapter Seven

PEACE

₤rratic man plunges blindly and alarmingly onward while the Guardians of Space stand by, assisting in many ways unknown to us, desiring always to give a helping hand to turn man aside from the yawning abyss his stumbling feet approach; desiring to 'steer him aright without taking the bull by the horns'. It is not their wish to use force or exhibit their powers unless absolutely necessary, but to serve their brother, to help him to bring peace and harmony to his world, for their motives are Universal in scope, not selfish.

Our Brothers, The Guardians, wisely remind us of the following words which are so little h e e d e d on Earth, "When evil speaks of good, be very careful how you accept it. Do not sit down with the devil to plan any good deeds for it will always be to benefit him!"

*Is there any viler hypocrisy than enemies of society pretending and preaching peace to those they would make their victims? Much more propaganda has been quoted in late years and many more con-

---
* Paul Jans, Wayside Wisdom on Hypocrisy, Brotherhood Truth Sheets, Vol. 63, No. 1 and No. 2.

ferences held than the number of times these two classics-for-directness uttered by Dr. Wesley Swift have been quoted: "Don't enter into any system to make the world good when you have to sit down with the devil to plan it." Also: "Beware when the devil teaches brotherhood."

Facing unhappy facts might be revolting to great numbers of people, but better to face them than to be overpowered by them to both the shame and chagrin of the many.

Hypocrisy has so devoutly mingled with religion that it is frequently mistaken for both religion and Truth. Hypocrisy loves disguise. Deceit ever masquerades as Truth, and propaganda is ever served up pleasantly to accomodate the thoughtless, and prejudice ever tries to tip the scales, while all three are easily peddled to the naive and indiscriminate without serving the scales of justice one particle.

In Matt. 23:28: "Even so ye also outwardly appear righteous unto men, but within ye are full of hypocrisy and iniquity." And today: At Diplomatic Conferences half of the world's distress is born at hypocritical conference foresworn.

We of America deceived ourselves when we allowed the gouged taxpayer to be exploited on a world-basis as a substitute for American statesmanship. Is it God's will that any nation or group of nations on Earth shall put God's people in colossal debt? Or is it the will of spurious leaders that have both denied and defied the will of God! In this country, the hatching of humanitarianism that is not also good Americanism is a hoax and a fraud.

Righteousness comes from peace; and complete honesty comes before charity. Far too great a portion of modern charity has developed into a world-wide humbug administered by do-gooder diligent hypocrites or idealists who sentimentally and hysterically tend to promote and perpetuate the very condition they pretend to be be curing. What a 'meanie' the spenders would think anyone who would make a statement like that!

Self-humbug may contain some slight degree of happiness in it, but hypocrisy nothing but shame, the little god, Stupidity. Who says the people of today have outgrown worshipping of idols since ancient times—idolaters of the stupidities of today?

In this country we cannot afford to turn to other 'isms,' ignore basically true American principles supported by Divine Law and trustfully worship wishy-willowing idealism in place of Yankee Doodle common sense. What fortress is worth reinforcing that none will defend! And we don't have to go beyond our own borders to find something worth defending. This country is worth saving right here at home.

The American people will either be the enactors of Principle not misconstrued with the expedience of edicts imposed by men, or collective followers of hypocrisy. For a generation or more at least, *they have chosen to follow hypocrisy and are today reaping* its bewildering rewards.

Americans should be reared not only to value pure honesty, but to see through distorters of the Truth in order not to willingly and witlessly serve dishonesty, hypocrisy, or unsuspectedly, their own destruction.

If hypocrisy and prejudice could be eliminated from human nature overnight, half the ills of the world would be conveniently *averted*, with little ado.

*There has been so much deceptive propaganda lately, particularly upon the subject of 'peaceful-coexistence' and even in some religious publications, that it might be just as well to generalize a little more on the subject of peace....

What the world calls peace is not peace. Peace, like love, is another very badly abused word in our language, and neither one is easy to grade or pinpoint, we must realize. There can only be peace during the absence of oppression. And time is not on our side without God. Certainly a peaceful coexistence plan to kid us into believing that it is, amounts to launching the world's biggest lie since the time of Adam and Eve. One might as well be given a time-bomb to hold, only to chant peace to drown out the sound of time ticking away while trustfully waiting for it to go off as to fall for that one, too. What have you given in appeasement each time the aggressor wants? Is that the best and only time to seek God's guidance? God does not require appeasement of us, but if there is anyone to whom we should surrender it is to Almighty God and not the enemy.

There is as much wisdom in the causal essence of peace as there is ignorance and misery in the blindnesses of war. And peace is more than a matter of guns silenced and slanted news. War will not end with the last bomb which falls or with the last shell which is fired. It will not only have to be fought to a finish, it will also have *to be thought* to a finish.

There are irreconcilable factions on one hand and another. Yet there is not peace, even less so, and *more and more unreasonable demands*. The pendulum of action and reaction has merely swung to

---
* Paul Jans, Pinpoints of Peace, Brotherhood Truth Sheets, 1956

the opposite extreme while ignoring balance and justice in that balance. When the clock of progress stops ticking it will be for total lack of all consideration for the rights of others. *There is no human peace outside the realm of right relations.* And right relations, both nationally and internationally, is more important than the planning and scheming of any power-hungry clique of one-worlders that can be gotten together anywhere on earth.

A declaration of Independence that is not as much for the people as for the government is not a government for the people but instead, a tyranny and degradation and subjugation of the just rights of either the people or of many peoples. Where pure principles are concerned, too much compromise means the demise and not the rise of a nation. Thank heaven there are still some individuals of sterling character left, both inside and outside of the Americas who will not agree to anything to make a questionable peace, or make salutations toward keeping a dangerously fictitious peace going. In peace or war, there can be no substitute for freeing the American people from known or undiscerned bondage. Any government whatever, which *denies its people the possibility of peace of mind*, will be continually in hot-water with crisis after crisis, deliberate or involuntary.

Major Tadao Watanabe refusing to indulge in double-talk, stated this year ('56) "We Japanese are not fooled by the peace talk of the Reds. We hope there will never be another war, but we know that peace means more than merely outlawing atomic bombs. Peace is like a table with four legs. They are liberty, justice, security, and brotherhood. Knock down any one of these legs, and the table falls. Yet Communism denies all four."

"It seems that peace conferences last longer than peace"—Pathfinder. It is easier to create dissension by talk than to assure peace thereby, for peace is much more than a matter of talk, past, present, or future. Winning peace on the battlefield only to lose it at the conference tables and in our hearts is a hollow victory. There is no freedom through a dishonorable peace worth having. Peace without honor would be worse than death. The Temple of Peace is built upon the foundation of righteousness, not upon the quicksands of talk. Expecting peace from prayers void of righteousness, is little more than a senseless dream. Dishonesty is faithless.

Physical comfort is important. Peace of mind is important. But greater than peace of mind is peace of soul, for peace of soul is greater than any mental confusion or intellectual tyranny on Earth. If the people and the leaders want peace, how is it then that they do not positively want complete righteousness and that they do not want and demand honesty and integrity from the top to the bottom and from the bottom to the top? For there can be no peace or security without righteousness. Righteousness and peace are for the most part reciprocal. There is no perfect peace without a full measure of sincerity, love, and purification.

An old Chinese proverb goes: "If there is righteousness in heart there will be beauty in character. If there is beauty in character there will be harmony in home. If there is harmony in home there will be order in nation. If there is order in nation there will be peace in world."

Politically speaking, most people today not only

don't want to know the truth, but won't believe it possible when they are told and hear it—and the worse the true facts which might be presented, the more difficult it is to persuade people to believe them. *Rather do they act as if there were more peace of mind to be had while being fooled than to know either the factual or the higher Truth.* And they seem not to want to trouble themselves to place 'peace of mind' upon a more permanent basis nor to care how soon it may vanish, just so they may have it for themselves while the having is good, regardless. Emotionally it is not the same as being at peace with one's self and therefore, at peace with the world, but rather an escapist-peace.

Were each and all willing and determined to contribute something purely good toward the general enlightenment, even though at first we but cast a lessening shadow, none would long be in darkness. Growing wiser while rightly motivated may take more initiative than to be fooled, but would yield less pain and tears for all.

If we do not industriously transform our character into something better during so-called peacetime, wars will deprive us of that fortunate privilege. Do we think we accomplish better through war what we failed to try to attempt while we had peace in which to do it? Is it not stupid to neglect duties in doing what is right during peace only to use all possible energy and skill during war to wreak wrong and destruction all because the preceding peace was misused? We might have simplified and improved every department of life for better and wiser living instead of resorting to wars, the nastiest way to clean house.

"I am the WAY, the Life and the Truth." These

are the Master's words. Many other ways are being substituted, but they are forever landing the human race into ruts, ruthlessness, crisis and confusions. It takes courageous strength of character, the most scrupulous integrity, delicate balance and self-control to deserve peace, and far more than a disgraceful ingratitude returned in exchange for a noble heritage or goodwill.

Peace would serve only the pure and just. How could paradise requite the corrupt? What may be proof to one may not be proof to another. Many who ask for proof before the harvest would do better to make themselves worthy of the fruit of the Spirit to realize the proof first-hand themselves, else they might doubt the harvest, before, or even after it appeared. Weak or faltering is the faith of him who always must have visible proof of the harvest before planting the seed or even preparing the ground.

Why should a brand of peace today be followed that must bring humiliation and our submission unto the ungodly tomorrow? Why not put the peace in action which will bring and insure peace tomorrow in body, heart, soul, and mind!

Chapter Eight

CONQUEST OF THE SKIES

Man has reached the point where if a thing is simple he completely overlooks it; if it is not complex it is of no value in his estimation, and cannot be a success. We could develop methods of flight much simpler and more effective if we would toss aside the sheer brute force of jet and rocket-propulsion—a fighting against laws of gravitational pull—for a natural force existing in the very air we breathe and everywhere present in the Universe, electro-magnetic f o r c e. Conversion would be much simpler if scientists would apply themselves and broaden their comprehension of natural principle, and far less expensive. At least man has not so far figured out a way to charge for the air he breathes.

Science knows that actual magnetic currents flow through everything, *a discovery that has destroyed everything science has postulated as a law.* In a few years such knowledge could enable man to do away with all present sources of power now commonly used such as oil, electricity, gas, coal, gasoline, etc. i.e., a little motor small enough to be inserted in the palm of the hand could be used to draw magnetic currents from the Earth itself, and run till it falls apart. Through the control of the magnetic currents we would gain unlimited power besides taking a colossal step forward in progress. In past highly developed civilizations of ancient times, man employed this natural power, sound and vibration, understanding and using Cosmic Laws. Why does present-day man hesitate? I leave the answer to you.

Arrogant and aggressive man shall find that his conquest of the skies cannot go beyond the heavi-side layer of this planet as long as he intends to go forth into outerspace to conquer other worlds, for the knowledge will not be given unto him. If he cannot enter outerspace with peace in his heart, and without being armed to the hilt, it is unlikely he'll ever discover the secret of interplanetary flight let alone make rocket missile tests without failure. Our present path of development will not reveal the secret.

> The eighth dimension of each planet (spoken of by scientists as the Heaviside layer) is of a different vibratory rate. This dimension surrounds each planet in a wall or globe of impenetrable force! [Impenetrable as far as man of this Earth is concerned.] The Heaviside layer of Earth ranges from twenty-eight to three hundred miles.* It holds the atmosphere to Earth, and keeps it from vanishing into outer space, acting as a boundary as well as protection. It acts as a buffer, or rather affords a

---

* The past few years and due to the incoming Earth cycle and the changes taking place throughout the Cosmos, the eighth dimension of our planet has expanded, moving outward several hundreds of miles.

protection for the Earth from invaders of outer space, such as meteors and beings that might be antagonistic to man. It is true that small meteors occasionally strike the surface of the earth, but they are only about one-millionth of their former size before coming through the Heaviside layer. The rate of vibration in the eighth dimension is such that it disintegrates material objects at an extremely rapid rate.

At once the thinking person will interrogate, "How then do the Brothers come through it to the Earth?"

In describing the means of propulsion that motivates their ships our Brothers explained that in order to penetrate the frequency of vibration of the heaviside layer, they blend the frequency of their ship with that which they enter into, by changing the polarity of the magnetic force-field generated and surrounding the ship.

To accomplish this a ship is so constructed that it draws in the electro-magnetic force of space (electro-magnetic or static-electricity everywhere present), converting or condensing it into a magnetic force-field or vortex which surrounds the ship. The radiation of this force-field decreases in pressure and intensity as it radiates outward from the ship, until it blends into space itself. The frequency of the vortex is controllable by instruments within the ship. Thus by generating their own polarity, becoming one with the atmosphere, and controlling gravity, they are not hindered in their space travel.

To explain further the means of propulsion that

motivates their ships, I quote from the book *Flying Saucers by* M. Doreal:

Magnetic currents flow throughout all the worlds and all space like rivers, so close together that there is one moving one way and one on another or slightly different river or vibratory octave so that by mere changing of a particular octave, a vessel motivated by it can move in any direction instantaneously. It can come to a dead stop, change its motion in another direction without there being any apparent braking power of any kind whatsoever.

When a ship is attuned to these magnetic currents it is not completely within this three-dimensional world. In other words, as soon as it begins to move on one of these magnetic currents it partially changes in dimensionality and as a result it is neither subject to the gravitational pull of the earth or to friction; it is not subject to material stress and strains and its movement is unlimited as long as it stays partially within the three-dimensional world, because during the time of its movement it immerses itself in the magnetic current and takes on a different dimensionality than the material world. That is the reason they can take on terrific speed and suddenly vanish because they have vanished not in space but in dimension.* They go to the second dimen-

---

* Dimensions in themselves are planes of comprehension. Each dimension is separate, a one dimensional plane, and on any plane we are limited in movement and direction only by our comprehension. We speak of the material world that we dwell in as a place of three dimensions, but in reality it is only a One dimensional world in which we have a concept of three dimensions. The higher dimensional planes are unlike the world of the senses, for movement upon them does not depend upon the functions of the senses. The ability to conceive of the different planes lies in the development of the inner mind or consciousness whose roots are buried in the Cosmic Mind."

sion, and in that state, movement or speed is practically instantaneous from one point to another.

Our Brothers are operating on an entirely different frequency or spectrum than we are here as third dimensional beings. I doubt that any ordinary person, scientist or physicist with what knowledge we have on this planet could operate one of their ships. Certainly not without their guidance, if at all. The secondary electro-magnetic principle is involved. The human body has to master the first degree of electro-magnetics. I am not speaking of primary electro-magnetics which, as you know, is man-made.

This Earth and all upon it has its existence in an all-pervading sea of electro-magnetic energy. We all live in, have our being in and operate in this sea of natural force, which is, at this present time, badly affected by the negative thought vibration of the mass-consciousness. This great universal power is universally distributed throughout all universes, and is the principle by which the Earth rotates, is the principle which holds the Earth in space, the primal secondary electro-magnetic force.

Magnetic electric currents are subtle, invisible currents that flow through *everything* in Nature. They have become the source of all the energies and powers that our Brothers use, not only to motivate their flying-ships and operate instruments, but which gives them power over all things in the animate world, the third dimension, and the second dimensional world. They know how to control them and release them in great power and force. They have oriented themselves into such a higher state that they may have control over life and death, over transfiguration and transmutation, thus applying this system of electro-magnetics to their own bodies, their own lives. If you develop your body to a high enough frequency by raising the state of your consciousness, you can levitate, walk on air, on the waters, just as Jesus the Christ did.

Our own Earth generates magnetic currents and our own bodies have magnetic energy flowing through them. Man is the center in which all these forces and currents are crossing and merging to try and find in him the perfect expression, the perfect channel, and for the reason that man is not a perfect channel, the perfect expression is not found and the force passes on. It depends on one's state of vibration how they intercept this power, how they take it on and how they use it as to whether they can, in turn, use it to manifest superhuman powers or to construct equipment that can absorb or draw in this secondary electro-magnetics and convert it to use in various forms, from motivating automobiles to supplying lighting systems.

Principles of secondary electro-magnetics is a vast study, and can be worked out whereby mankind can be greatly benefited. These electro-magnetic forces and principles are free for anyone to utilize, being all-pervading, everywhere present. The keys to these things are now available to those who seek them. These natural, universal forces must not be employed in any negative, destructive manner, but only for the highest good.

Our Brothers can be called the Watchers of this planet, and, of course, other worlds. If a knowledge of the electro-magnetic forces and principles are used destructively they can offer opposition by immediately nullifying the force, then those with evil intent cannot accomplish their purpose.

It is quite obvious that what man of Earth believed yesterday to be true does not apply to today. And ever it shall be as long as he continues to make the effort to grow in knowledge and wisdom. But, how can he believe he is growing or progressing when he calamitously condones in destructive preparation which can only prevent growth, and that may rob us of a future? The things being done are but barbaric and outside the pale of civilization.

The world today, as a matter of fact, is in a lesser degree of civilization than it has been many times in the ages past. "But", you may exclaim vehemently, "That cannot be! We are civilized."

But are we? If the world were civilized would there be crimes, torture, mass murder, false doctrines, etc.? Since war, hatred and intolerance are major factors in the life of man, he is uncivilized. He has not advanced very much in the last two thousand years, having only learned to use more of the laws of nature for his own comfort. As far as his spiritual growth and awareness are concerned he has made little progress.

Never were truer words spoken or writ than 'Man, know thyself and thou will know all things,' for this saying contains within itself the germ of all truth. When man knows himself, then and only then can he know God. Until he does he can never travel the great spaceways. He can never be free of the bondage of this little 'speck of dust' called Earth. Man, a finite creature because he is unbalanced on the finite p l a n e which causes him to be bound in the physical body, is limiting himself by the three dimensional world around him. All of his concepts are bound up within that limitation. If a person thinks of rising up into the skies and going higher and higher, the human mind cannot conceive of the illimitable Space-mind.

It is impossible for the third dimensional, mathematical mind to conceive of endless space or solve its mysteries. Our mathematical speculations upon space are third dimensional attempts to rationalize a higher dimensional geometry. The explanation of the fact that the Great Void is truly endless and just as truly bounded (not limited) lies in the expansion and contraction of the Void, and that it is absolute space.

The finite mind, being illusion-clouded, p i c t u r e s space entirely different from what it is. The mind recognizes space as apart from itself because of its unconsciousness of the Oneness of itself with space. We live in mind-space, one with the Cosmic. "Cosmic Mind is space and space is Cosmic Mind, moving in an ordered procession of movements. Our consciousness of the Cosmic is a part of the Cosmic Consciousness of itself. There is no existence of anything except in this consciousness." We cannot reach the limits of space by reaching out beyond or by counting millions of light years, but by turning our thoughts toward the Cosmic Mind, then we will find space and infinity in One.

We can attain to the higher only by spiritual growth and awareness. Only by our development of consciousness here on this planet can we become ready for a higher planet. Such development is brought about by experience and desire, by turning to the true, inner man, the spiritual man. This does not mean you must eliminate all material things from your life. All the sages of all religions have taught that man must become spiritual because Jesus said, "God is spirit and must be worshipped in spirit and truth", a passage which is quite overworked. Man is made not in a physical image of God, but in the spiritual image of God.

Man should realize that he is not a child of God, but is, in his highest nature, God itself. 'God itself' because He is neither male nor female. God is all things; He is One. There is nothing without Him, nothing in all the universe which is not God. Even negation or that which man calls evil, is God which is in a condition of inharmony in relation to the perfect order of God. Man, himself, is a fallen God, yet he is still a channel through which Divine Order seeks to perfect negative disorder. Every experience we can conquer perfects some of the disorder into a condition of perfect order which results in growth and expansion of Divine Light.

Many have a wrong conception of God. Living in a world of form and substance they are accustomed to measure God by their own idea of form and substance. They say that He is perfect; they say that He is the absolute of all there is and they are correct in that in a way, but it is nature for the material mind to limit God. They think of Him as all perfection and there is nothing beyond that perfection. Have you ever thought that what is perfection to man is not perfection to God? If God is a living spirit, He is a growing spirit and He cannot be limited in any circle, even perfection. If that were true then God could not think a new thought, He could not create anything new. The Ancient's concept of God was: "That He was ever growing, ever expanding, ever becoming greater and greater and all His parts were growing into an ever greater state." The idea of an anthropomorphic God was established because man mistook the symbol for the real and brought Him down to Earth and applied all their own attributes to Him. That is why we read in the Old Testament that God was a jealous God, and that He repented. Man fell from his high estate and he repented and he thought God repented. That is the way with people, we try to blame things on someone else, and man must eradicate that condition from his consciousness for it is not until we know ourselves that we can know God for we are the reflection of that great light.*

---

*Light can be described as a composite of the Soul's Wisdom. The human organism is connected with its Soul by a ray of ineffable Divine Light. The Light in the average person is only slightly expressed, as he is not conscious that it exists. The light must be set into motion; it must flow through the individual to become a reality, and not just a potentiality.

Chapter Nine

WHY DON'T 'THEY'?

Some of the more common queries often repeated are "Why don't 'they' come openly to communicate with us?" "Why don't 'they' teach us? What is their purpose, anyway?"

Our Brothers have told me, "It would not be easy for your people to understand our purpose. The creator is all in One, and the same in All Vastness. We are all working as One." Their purpose in life is to continually grow in knowledge, seeking always to change into order that which has been disordered, knowing that in living and purifying experiences and things, they add to the perfect light of that of the Divine. Their every thought and deed is to please and obey the will of the Creator, doing all things lovingly. Can men of Earth truthfully admit as much?

These beings of sister planets, our Brothers, are not coming to Earth to create phenomena, to appear in your front yard just to please you or satisfy your curiosity, or to purposely create any disturbance of any kind, or to deliberately interfere with our governments or our way of life. Their ships in our skies are significant of friendship and brotherhood. If this were not the case they could have taken us over lock, stock and barrel long ago and without a struggle. Since they understand Universal Laws and know how to employ them, they could easily change conditions on Earth. They could bring war and aggression to an end as far as physical manifestation is concerned, and in moments of time, but *as long as these things are in the heart of man it would be of no avail to remove them from the outer world.* They know only too well that man's destiny lies within man's own self, and therefore they do not come into our world to force mankind to become as they are, *for no one can become what they do not desire of their own free will.*

Their major purpose in coming is not only scientific, but also to alert man to the need of understanding himself, knowing himself for what he really is; of becoming aware of potent, dormant faculties lying in wait, within the inner man, to be awakened. We must remember that our Brothers have their lives to live and to fulfill, striving for improvement, and problems to be met, too, yet they are willing to take time out from their own advancement to extend a helping hand to their stumbling brothers living in darkness. They do not compel any man into any way of life, therefore they desire only to help those who desire to become more perfect channels for the manifestation of Divine Law; to help those climbing the ladder to at-one-ment with the Divine.

It is not their objective to teach us at present for we must first help ourselves to advance by beginning to live with more respect toward each other, and help ourselves to unfold by making an attempt to tap the unused reservoirs of power lying deep within us. We must make an effort to lift ourselves out of our present state of self-consciousness into the real immortality of Cosmic Consciousness.* They are not interested in the personal problems of our everyday life; they are interested in our spiritual growth, in humanity as a whole, and therefore, it is their purpose to give us guidance and counsel if we will but accept it. Thus they refer us to the highest source of truth teachings available on our planet—*teachings of universal principle true throughout the Universe and on all other planets.* This that we may gain a clear and detailed understanding of the real nature of man, that we may regain the Spirituality which was once ours, that each who so desires may play his part in bringing forth the Kingdom of Heaven or Holy City on Earth, that ultimately Universal Peace will reign throughout the Cosmos. Man must first seek the Kingdom of Heaven within himself before the Christ Kingdom can be established here on our planet. "Man must create an inner harmo-

---
* Cosmic Consciousness is the result of growth—not some sudden power. It is a knowledge of the life, law and order of the Universe— a knowing that everything is a part of the universal law and that All life is merely a unified division of the Whole. We are aware that before time existed we were; and after time we will be. That we are Creator and created."

EMBLEM OF PLUTO

ny and understanding, and reflect the Christ-light into the outer material world." Our Brothers know that the Kingdom will not be brought in without a terrific struggle in the heart and soul of man, for many there are who love darkness and will take their stand in opposition and rejection. They know this Earth is a prison world with many rebel souls, and as long as they, the rebel souls, have an intense desire for power, dominance, and destruction, that long will the struggle, the battle exist.

Validated records have been kept of strange objects that have been seen in the skies for centuries by competent observers in Europe, Asia, America and other places. The Earth has been watched for a long time by races of other worlds, though it is not the only planet that has been under observation, even in other systems. For a long period of time this globe of ours has been quarantined.

Our Brothers bid me with deep, impressive feeling, "You may tell your people we would like to be welcome to come openly, and not in secrecy as we have to plan." How can they come among us freely when there is rampant in man's being a desire for power and dominance over his fellow man? When we are a hostile people under military control? How can they come freely when the public has not prepared itself to accept them openly, either believing there are no other inhabited worlds, or if so, God positively would not permit the inhabitants to come to this Earth; or, if there is some sort of life form existent on other planets, then it either has not the intelligence to invent and propel a spacecraft to Earth or if so, they could only be monsters and their intentions anything but peaceful? Hence, how can our Brothers come openly when the enamored multitudes, *satisfied with belief rather than knowledge*, do not understand that *our danger lies here on Earth with man himself*, but prefer to believe that they, our Brothers, are the menace? Man has sought the lower, and the world, rather than the higher and spiritual and that which is beyond the world. Therefore, our Brothers do not come openly and freely among us in a quarantined world.

It can be said they do not come among us freely for the same reason that the Great White Lodge has stayed apart from the world. There are some people who wonder why those of the lodge do not come forth to help a chaotic world. These Great Ones or Elder Brothers are not material rulers, but spiritual rulers; they are guides of mankind. They remain hidden from the world at large for if material man could find his way to them the masters would have to spend all their time protecting themselves from power-mad men endeavoring to obtain the secrets they have. The Great Ones are custodians of knowledge, and man must earn the right to it.

It is being written in books and filmed for the movies that Flying Saucers do exist but their home is not the Earth. However, it all depends on what type of UFO is being referred to. Readers and movie-goers are being led astray with half-truths and fallacies which are dangerous as well as misleading. The documented picture 'UFO'S', released in theaters throughout the country the summer of 1956 was, I believe, the first factual showing of its kind. Though it did not reveal too much, it was a refreshing change from the fare of silence or denial to which the public has been subjected, in that it was admitted the UFO'S are real, they do exist, that they are solid objects, not birds or balloons or hallucinations or reflected lights, that they are not anything the United States is either experimenting with or producing, and as far as they know, no other country is producing any. I might add that the United States and other countries own a number of types of modern planes that are kept secret from the public, and are similar in appearance to so-called Flying Saucers, and have been mistaken for them.

However, let us recall the movie "Earth vs. the Flying Saucers". This is a typical picture that implies danger lies from invasion from outer-space, in this instance from an asteroid belt, when in actuality, the source of our only definite menace is here *on our own Earth*. You will find that out some day.

As you probably know, the name Flying Saucer is a misnomer, having been applied as early as 1947 to any unaccountable object observed in the skies, since there were those sighted that appeared to look like up-side down saucers. The Air Force has chosen to call these "Flying Saucers" Unidentified Flying Objects or UFO for short.

It should be disclosed to and understood by the public that there are a number of UFO besides the U.S. craft that have been mistaken for them. They can be grouped in three groups and said to originate from three sources. One, interplanetary, or the cylindrical and round or globular objects. Two, the interdimensional, or triangular or pyramid shaped objects, and three, the earthly or disk-shaped objects. The various kinds are seldom seen together as they are carrying out entirely different purposes.

The interdimensional or triangle shaped objects that have been seen at times, have appeared to have several circles of light around them and to glow red. Our world, though it may be difficult for you to believe, is not the only inhabited place. In the dimensions of space between planets and other solar systems there are beings who live just as there are dwellers upon other worlds. The triangle or pyramid shaped objects are from the interlocking world space that is relative to this world of ours. They are farther advanced than we are in general, and have a knowledge our scientists do not possess as yet. Though our atomic explosions have damaged their realms considerably, there is no danger from them.

The interplanetary type that I and others have been contacting are from higher evolved planets. These great superconstructions are called "Mother Ships" and "Spanners", and are carriers of small 'scout ships' or cruising craft which are commonly used to travel within the atmosphere of a planet. Those who travel in these craft are divinely appointed Watchers or Guardians of space, being given charge over the lesser worlds, to guard them from harm. They guard against lower evolved worlds striking against another. There are antagonistic denizens of some not-so-highly evolved worlds who would like nothing better than to invade the Earth and aid the anti-christ during Armageddon. Spiritually, man of Earth, has not advanced, while scientifically and mechanically he has moved rapidly forward during the past century. He is not ready for the giant weapon he holds in his child-like hands. The growing power of material science and technology may destroy his spiritual foundations and civilization itself, but he will not be permitted to pass to other worlds and carry that destruction with him.

The earthly, or disk-shaped objects have been seen over most every country, and particularly in places where work dealing with nuclear materials for weapons purposes is concerned. These cannot be classified as friendly. They are not of the friendly Martians, Jupiterians, and other planet people coming to Earth with friendly intentions. Regardless of what some people, some books, and some movies may imply, there is no danger of attack from outerspace from our Brothers of other planets in this system, but rather much necessitated succor when and as needed, and in conformity with Cosmic Law.

There are those who question our need of outside assistance, claiming that we have God to pray to for deliverance. But who are we to question or say how our prayers shall be answered? Are we not all agreed that the Creator is the All-Knower? Can we then, rightfully, say the source of help will not come through people of other planets, the Creator's helpers, who obey His Will explicitly, not personal will as we do? When human efforts have been so insufficient to cure the ills of the world, what better way than to send His Children of higher culture, evolution and wisdom to aid their lowly brothers for whom they have great tolerance, love and compassion, much as a parent for an erring child who has not yet learned right from wrong and brings harm to himself or another. Who could be more capable of directing and guiding us than these elder Brothers who long ago trod the same path we are now? They know how badly we shall need their counsel and assistance before the Time of Trouble has passed away, for as they have told me, "Mundane beings of Earth do not understand how to receive help from or commune with their Creator, and most all of their churches are misled!" Instead of showing man what would happen if he lived in accord with Divine Law, the churches have taught fear and hell. There are those that have preached Christ, and instigated hate. Through fear and hate no lasting gains can be made either by individuals or nations. The only lasting gain is that made by doing the right thing at the right time, with the right purpose and the right understanding. It was never intended that any one group of people or race or religion should ever rule the world and enslave others. The multitudes are too immersed in and bound by authority, dogma, custom, and above all, by *fear* to realize there are Universal Laws operating on unchanging, unbreakable principle. It is true that the only law man can break is the law he himself has made; he cannot break Divine Law, but is continually breaking himself against it.

The African savage sacrifices his enemy and eats a piece of his heart to gain courage and strength. In communion, some of the Christian churches are symbolically doing the same thing, not realizing that actual communion should be one of the Spirit and needs no outer symbol. To literally enter into true communion is to live and think that one becomes a channel for Truth, Wisdom and Divine Law to manifest through. The flesh and blood spoken of symbolically by Jesus to be partaken of in communion was the Truth he taught which man must make an absolute part of himself before he can find God. The famished religions of Christendom should be abandoned for true spiritual food that is free from tradition, and orthodox theology.

A lot of us enter into prayer without preparing ourselves for prayer. The power of prayer is in accordance with an individual's contact with the inner Source of Light and Love in the very depth of his own being. Many prayers are never answered and we wonder why. Occasionally and by chance we get results from time to time yet not having a clear understanding of what we are doing. It is because we do not realize that we cannot approach God in a condition of negation.

"The very nature of inharmonious consciousness repulses the Divine principle from manifesting through your nature. God is calm, and peaceful, and quiet, and still, and you can only attune yourself with the Divine when you create a like condition in your own mind and consciousness. All you have to do is to harmonize yourself with God so you can become a channel through which He can express the things which are necessary for your well-being. It means sitting down calmly, quietly, dismissing all things from your mind, all your troubles and worries, making your mind become as still and quiet as a pool of water that is not disturbed by a single ripple and then in your own inner self, with all the power and strength of your mind, desire that you commune with and attune yourself with the Divine Spirit.

To do that you have to retire into your secret chamber—the cave of the brain, the point at which God manifests to you. Our conscious mind might be said to be the guardian of the doorway to that inner chamber. Before we enter we must enter into the Silence. Entering the silence does not mean just having a place where you can be alone and silent, but literally this, that we are to shut off from our consciousness all of the things of the active, external or material world.

If you have approached the gateway in calmness and quietness, with your purpose and thought pure, and desiring with all your power to commune, you are ready to pronounce The Word* that opens the gate, the power going upward and the power going downward from the Divine, then with all your might just try to allow your mind to become as still and blank as possible.

One should not commune with God to gain power, money, or health. You need not ask for something. In so doing you will limit your supply. Just have the deep desire to enter into communion with Him, remembering what Jesus the Christ said, "Be not ye therefore like unto them, for your Father knoweth what things ye have need of before ye ask for them." The Divine Spirit is ever pressing against us seeking a way to enter and manifest through us. If we will commune and attune ourselves with God so there will be an

---

* The Word is not some magic word; it is a vibration which is neither material nor immaterial but is rather a balancing of the two. The Word is the changing of your consciousness to such a state of harmony of thought and thinking that the Divine Power can find a means of attunement with your own inner nature. It was through vibration that the Divine created things, that all things came into being through and by The Word, and The Word was the audible expression of the vibratory creative power of the Divine."

open door to enter, we will be that channel for Him to manifest through. If a person once establishes perfect communion, nothing that is disturbing or harmful in any way will ever come to their life thereafter. Man as an individual and as a mass has the right to establish that communion with the Divine Spirit. In so doing they would find paths in life opening to them that they never dreamed existed.

Chapter Ten

VISIT WITH THE BROTHERS

After eight months of many pleasant and inspirational subjective contacts, my cherished expectation was fulfilled; I at last had my first objective meeting alone with a being from another world.

On this particular night I was reading a publication from the BROTHERHOOD OF THE WHITE TEMPLE, INC., when I realized I had missed a regular evening TV program. The next thing I noticed was that the light on the porch went out. I had a strange indescribable feeling, and arose and went out the door to check the light bulb, reasoning that it must have burned out. A friendly, pleasing voice spoke to me from the darkness, "Please do not turn the light on, my brother." Then I saw him, not too clearly in the dim light of the night, standing about twenty feet away. I walked toward him with no sense of apprehension whatsoever. He accosted me with a particular mode of hand-clasp used by people of other planets, and I greeted him, inviting him to come in, and later wondered how I'd had the presence of mind to say anything at all, so overcome was I.

In all the telepathic and physical contacts, the feeling these Brothers and Sisters arouse is always one of peace, harmony and love, pouring forth from them, striking a responsive chord in my own being. So much is said and sung on this Earth about love, but I daresay that few have known the true meaning of true love until they stand in the presence of those who are open channels for the Divine Love of the Creator to flow through. This kind of Love is difficult for people to understand for it is sufficient unto itself and needs nothing but a means of expression. It is a joy that knows no bounds. It defies definition, and I find myself at a total loss to adequately define it, for who can define the Infinite? The potency of such Divine Love will temper the hearts of men and exemplify their lives, creating a new sense of fellowship in which men of all nations will build the sort of world in which the tragedies of yesterday cannot be repeated.

Now, standing alone in the presence of this highly evolved Brother from another planet, I perceived this profound feeling to be so very much more intense than during mental telepathy contacts, that a great surge of humility welled up within me, and involuntarily I began to kneel before him. He took hold of my arm with a restraining hand, avowing, "That is all right, my brother. Where I come from all are equal."

When I asked if I might know what planet he came from he merely replied, "Not at this time." It was only recently that it was confided to me that he and the Brother who accompanied him on an ensuing visit are from a planet in our solar system, but that the planet is non-existent to the people of Earth since our astronomers have not as yet discovered it. One precise fact was revealed at this first meeting, and that is that even though our Brothers are truthfully so much farther advanced intellectually and spiritually, they do not express any feeling of superiority. All are equal; all are respected alike. *Regardless of race, color, creed or education all are One with the Creator.* And although, in our sense of the word, they are gods, they would not have us think or speak or bow down to them as such.

I marveled at his keen extra-sensory perception, for although he had not accepted my invitation to come in, he was quite aware of what I had been reading at the time of his arrival, commenting on "the good literature you are reading." He also commended me for keeping my faith.

All too soon he announced, "I must go now, my dear brother." Entreatingly I spoke, "I hope to see you again soon, my brother." In a daze and with tears in my eyes I turned away as he blended into the night. I did not even think of the darkened light bulb until some minutes after his departure and I had returned to my room, when it lit up as though an unseen hand had turned it on.

Since then I have had many soul-inspiring visits,

each a memorable experience, with these benevolent people, and have especially come to know those from the planets Pluto and Jupiter. Their visits are always for a purpose and never for idle pastime. Nevertheless, do not let me give you the wrong impression, for they are naturally a happy, effervescent people. I've merited the privilege of being present at a few of their council meetings, and despite the seriousness of the moment or any slight disagreement that might arise, always the greatest of compatability prevails with an atmosphere of peace, harmony and good will, which would put to shame any meeting ever held by people of Earth.

For two nights a week, following this contact, I observed a craft circle overhead, and move erratically as if putting on a display of maneuvers. Another week passed by and late one night, on awakening, I turned over and looking out the window I saw a ship traveling southward, not too fast. As it disappeared from view, I fervently wished that I could see it again. A few seconds later, and much to my surprise, here it came back into view and hovered a moment or two. It appeared to be about as large as a dinner plate, although its actual size I could not estimate. A mental impression came through without the usual opening and closing words, "We are pleased we have some sincere observers. May see you later."

And indeed, a week later I was honored by a visit from the same Brother who came before, and this time he was accompanied by another Brother, a well-built man, too, but of taller stature, probably six feet one inch in height. The iridescent material of their form-fitting garments, similar in style to our ski-suits, was unusually soft to the touch, firm but beautifully textured. The colors were what we refer to as the blue-violet shades. They were fine looking men, with smooth, dark sun-tan complexions, and dark hair styled in longer length than our modern cuts. Their footwear appeared to be most sturdy though having no openings.

This night their arrival* was preceded by a restlessness on my behalf. Considering the darkness outside, the light filtering through the windows seemed unreal. I stepped onto the front porch as if drawn there by a magnet, and immediately saw them standing nearby. They accepted my invitation to come in.

Among other things, they spoke of our leaders, our people, the Creator and of Nature. The tallest one repeated the following in a rhythmical flow, and with profound meaning, every word holding me spellbound, afterwards explaining that "it has not been given to anyone on your planet before. It is yours to do with as you wish:

---

* You will note that throughout my story I have not mentioned any place of contact. For reasons you may well understand, since there are those desirous of domination and oppression, it is neither wise, nor the proper time to reveal the whereabouts of any place I have met with the Brothers from other planets. Of far greater import is their message of truth, guidance and friendship!

Accept thy brothers and sisters from the land—
The Creator will give thy hand.
   Learn thyself from the heart—
   The Creator will do thy part.
You will then know Nature and become free;
You will know what to do when you come to Thee."

At first glance it may seem like simple nonsense but if you apply reason and logic combined with a bit of concentration it will disclose worlds of meaning.

During the interim between this contact and the next one three weeks later, I saw quite a little activity in the skies. Also on the thirteenth and the eighteenth of the month of November there was a fall of so-called 'angel-hair' floating through the air and clinging to the buildings, trees, and electric power-lines. I understand this 'angel-hair' is a waste product expelled from the Mother Ships or Carriers, and produced by a process of mass conversion of positive and negative electrons of the magnetic force field of a primary nature at a time of necessary repair work, when an emergency unit of propulsion is in operation.

My next physical contact was a startling one. I had been in contact via the inner-voice with this Brother and Sister from Jupiter whom I now was privileged to meet in person. I recognized the pleasing tone of his voice at once, but I had not anticipated meeting a woman, especially one with such exquisite beauty as I

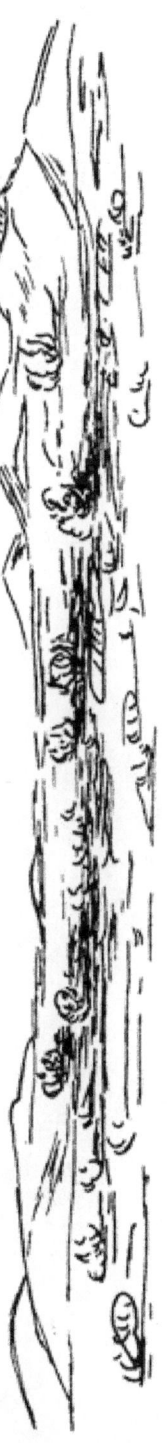

JUPITER CRUISER

now beheld. She greeted me warmly as I stood there amazed and dumbfounded. Her voice was perfectly modulated. "We only stopped by for a few moments. I wanted to see you." She warned me to be careful in what I believed, to accept only what I knew to be the Truth, and to set aside whatever I doubted. "If it is truth it will come to you as such when the time is right."

At last, finding I was not completely speechless, I ventured to ask her a question which had been bothering me. "There are a lot of different versions of Jesus' life. I would like to know the truth about it. Will you tell me?"

Her answer was, "You have a book; if you will study it, you will learn what you wish to know." On this occasion they did not come in, and the only book I had in my room at this time was *The Textbook of Ancient Wisdom* by M. Doreal, yet she had, as had the Brother of a previous meeting, the uncanny ability of knowing without seeing with material eyes. I had only commenced to read this book, and the next morning I picked it up and involuntarily turned to page thirty-four on which, at a glance, I found as follows, what I desired to know:

"The true master can enter into the spirit of the things the people around him are doing, regardless of what it might be. He can drink with the drinker, gamble with the gambler, and yet not be touched with the destructive vibration like them, for he knows that only by placing himself on their level can he hope to raise them to his own plane. That is why the Master, Jesus, was known as a consorter with sinners and Publicans; that is why men called Him a drunkard and glutton. He was able to enter any atmosphere without condemnation of the things that were being done. He knew, as all who have come into Mastership know, that the only sin is that committed, when one who knows refuses to give the true seeker the knowledge of how to reach the goal.

Christ consorted with so-called sinners, because He knew that only by being with them could He lift them out of their darkness. It was this He meant when He said, 'If I be lifted up, all men shall be drawn unto me.'"

This Brother's wearing apparel was form-fitting though permitting freedom of movement, the top, waist-length, and similar in style to our 'flight' jackets, although I could detect no buttons or zippers. The Lady of Jupiter wore a fashionable skirt and blouse with a jacket. I caught a glimpse of what appeared to me to be an insignia on her blouse.

Indicating they must go, they turned to leave and I accompanied them a short distance, then they warmly bid me goodbye, and our Sister repeated in soft cadence:

> "The Wind is your anger,
> The Sun is your body,
> The Moon is your heart,
> A Star is your soul."

She added, "Study it, my dear brother. It will also be good for your mate" (wife). Though not another word was spoken, I knew I must walk no farther with them. As they neared a dark object wrapped in the dim cloak of night, a faint shaft of light showed from it. Moments later it grew brighter, the whole craft glowing blue, then reddish-orange as it lifted. As it arose into the night sky the color lightened, changing to a bluish shade again. At first it appeared to rise vertically for possibly a thousand feet, then took off on perhaps a forty-five degree angle. At a much greater height, it made a circle, then headed eastward, now traveling at a tremendous speed, appearing as a blue-white streak amongst the stars. And there I stood, lost to this world, and wishing with all my heart and soul that I was aboard that swiftly receding ship.

Succeeding this meeting I was contacted clairaudiently or by the inner voice, and still later complimented with a visit in person from the mettlesome and lovely little Lady of Pluto, the one who had spoken with me at Giant Rock. She is about five feet three inches tall, and on this occasion wore a blouse, jacket and slacks in contrasting tones of a beautiful, pansy-blue, similar to royal blue, and a shade of red-wine in a scintillating, deep intensity. She was most pleased that I recognized her. It was a pertinent remark she made and the familiarity of her smooth, mellow voice which revealed her identity to me. That day at Giant Rock, in order to avoid attracting undue attention, she had cleverly disguised her flawless complexion with make-up and freckles, as well as controlling to a necessary degree the vibrant harmonies that radiate from her being.

I had not previously met the Brother who accompanied her, and who presently took a leaf of paper from my notebook on the table and drew the insignia that was designed upon his shirt and her blouse in a golden yellow hue. He asked if I could draw it, and I made a rough sketch which he said would do. However, he folded and slipped his copy into his trouser's pocket. This insignia was the emblem of the planet Pluto which is illustrated in this book for your scrutiny, along with the emblem of Jupiter. These cannot be considered exact duplicates, being more or less drawn from memory.

This little Lady of Pluto quoted in cadent diction the following prayer to be given to my mate and her good friend, M——. However, it was about two weeks later before it became obvious that it was a quote. "Mighty Spirit of Light, that shines through the Cosmos, draw my flame closer in harmony to Thee. Lift up my fire from out of the darkness, magnet of fire that is One with the All.'" An active member of our study group obtained a copy of the Emerald Tablets of Thoth, The Atlantean, published by the BROTHERHOOD OF

THE WHITE TEMPLE, INC.* Without having read it herself, she handed it to me that I might do so. Before beginning the book I flipped the pages, pausing to read aloud a passage here and there. In a few minutes I was repeating familiar words, the prayer that the Lady of Pluto had spoken.

In continuing I will add as an explanation that the two Sisters, one a representative of the planet Pluto and the other of the Planet Jupiter, are what we would refer to in rank as captains, although they render other services besides piloting a ship. I questioned the captain or Lady of Pluto, "Is it true that women are captains on all the spaceships?" to which she answered, "We do not have classification in rank as your people do. [No captains, no colonels, lieutenants or generals, etc.] We are all equal; all are respected alike no matter what services they perform. Our attainments and capabilities vary. Some Brothers are in charge of ships, and some Sisters, according to their advancement in spiritual growth."

I rejoined with another question, "Do you have maids and servants?" and she replied, "There are some who like to render service in the homes of others, but

---
* The Brotherhood of the White Temple was founded by Dr. M. Doreal and established in Sedalia, Colorado. "It is a channel, of the Masters, in direct connection with the Great White Lodge, being chosen as one of the paths through which sincere selfless seekers, willing to dedicate their lives to the service of mankind may prepare themselves for the coming of the new spiritual World Teacher, the Incarnation of the Christ-Consciousness."

do not remain in the same home indefinitely. What you refer to as labor, we undertake lovingly. Our people all rule their planet together for the common good of all, each playing his essential role. All have freedom of choice, and all have the opportunity to visit other planets."

As a Brother told me during an earlier meeting, "On our planet we do a job, we do it well. We do not have to go back and do it over again." Have we of Earth achieved the ability to do things right the first time? Everybody knows that the first automobile, the first airplane, the first radio, as well as the first mousetrap were not built right. Surely we must question the nuclear fission research experiments. Man might at least do better than to allow so much human intelligence to go generally to waste.

This was January 1955, and the Lady of Pluto's next disclosure smote me with astonishment, "There is a small planet that has moved from its normal orbit and is circling closer to the Earth. There may be many strange feelings. Do not become alarmed; it will be handled dexterously. The most critical conditions are yet to come upon Earth; there will be many changes in many ways."

She continued, briefly explaining that by their knowledge of working with and by natural and spiritual law this planet would be regulated and kept safely on its course, unless it should become too unbalanced through natural processes, in which event they would not intercede with Nature's operations; the laws of Nature would hold sway, governing its activity. Our Brothers will not set aside any workings of Law, but only harmonize their purpose to that working. Natural law shares in the preservation of balance, and to attempt to divert natural law results in instant manifestation. They know there can be no violation of natural material law or spiritual law if an ordered existence is to be expected; there must be a perfect balance and harmony established and maintained.

To my knowledge, no mention was made publicly at the time of this planetoid's minor declination, except by a TV program, and according to this program such an occurrence was apparently expected sometime in the near future. The first printed news brought to my attention much later, was a short item published in the Los Angeles Times Newspaper, dated November, the twenty-sixth, 1956, in which it was stated to be a tiny asteroid that was expected to collide with the Earth in '69, and that it is much closer to the Earth than any other heavenly body except the moon.

Our Brothers indisputably maintain that our astronomical findings are miscalculated as to distance, size, and atmospheric conditions of other bodies in space, and the theory of collision is also erroneous. They assert there is no human life existent on the planetoid, and that our scientists are unaware of the innumerable heavenly bodies within our solar system as they have not as yet explored it with any certainty. They concluded that we need not be concerned with any collision; there are far more serious matters at hand to consider and cope with!

It is my hypothesis that our astronomers were not aware of this so-called asteroid moving towards the Earth's orbit in early 1955, or if they did detect it was off its usual course, they certainly did not suspect it was under control. Won't you take a moment to lift your eyes and gaze out into the wild blue yonder of space? Are you not awe-struck with the wonder of still being here? Let us give thanks to the Guardians of Space, the Guardians of Earth. How little we know, how little we appreciate these, our neighbors, our Brothers and Sisters from other worlds!

Scientists miscalculate distances because they do not understand the different dimensions of space. The many stars we see are not as far distant as our astronomers theorize; it is because we see their reflections through angled space dimensions that they appear so distant. For instance, the sun is much closer than 93,000,000 miles, being several millions of miles less in distance from the Earth.

All stars do not have planets surrounding them, but since there are an immense number of stars, if only one in a hundred thousand had planets revolving around it, there would still be an unthinkable number. Second-dimensional channels connect every star with every other star. These channels blend with the eighth dimension of each as well as interpenetrating the ninth dimension of space between planets and stars. To explore the 'limitations' of space we must follow the lines of extension or second dimensional passages.

Though space dimension is but one—extension, this extension is endless, unlimited and of several dimensions within itself, interpenetrating each other. These different dimensional planes are not strata or layers one above the other, but are octaves of vibration, seperated only by those octaves of vibration, yet interpenetrating each other in every point of space. "A plane of being is not a place, but a state of being."

It may be difficult to conceive of more than one manifestation occupying the same point of space at the same time. Students of physics know that any point in space may contain vibration of light, gas, heat, electricity, magnetism, and other more subtle energies. Every color is contained in rays of sunlight, and these rays can be separated into their component parts. Light passes through window glass, yet both occupy the same space, and are separated by rates of vibration so that one does not affect the other.

Though space is invisible it is filled with waves of energy and electrified 'dust' particles. Moving within space are natural forms of different densities activated by the ether waves. Ether of space has always been in dispute among scientists, being little understood. The basic substance of ether is Cosmic Dust from which electrons are builded and from which all things are created. All planets are born and formed out of the electrified 'dust' particles of space.

Energy and light are inseparable. Light can be said to flow through all space, thrown off by the sun as high velocity particles, being transmitted not so much in waves as in particles like the transformer that reduces the voltage of electricity. If the mighty energy of the sun were poured forth, reaching the earth unchecked, destruction would be inevitable. The sun is the positive polarity of this system and it is a center of energy constantly radiating through space, carrying particles of matter on its radiation.

Astronomical theories lead us to believe that there is no air on the moon. However, the internal pressure of a heavenly body and the external pressure strike a perfect balance, else a moon or planet would disintegrate. The outer pressure is none other than the atmosphere surrounding the form in its movement through space. Our moon, being small, has a lighter atmosphere than the Earth, but not too light for people of other planets to live there.

Government officials and scientists are sure the moon has a life-supporting atmosphere else they would not hope to reach it. It is said the first nation to land there

146

ERRATUM—page 146

Paragraph one: The second sentence should read—
Light can be said to flow through all space, thrown off by the sun as high velocity particles *at varying speeds. The natural ether acts upon these particles* like the transformer that reduces the voltage of electricity.

and fly its flag will rule the Earth. If we are wise we will attempt to reach the moon with peace and friendliness in our hearts, for it is the domain of a happy, peace-loving people, and we will not be permitted to usurp it.

There is a vast center or hub of this Cosmos around which all galaxies and solar systems move, and through this hub pours the radiating power and energy that quickens and makes alive this Cosmos. Solar systems are only atoms in the Cosmos, in the Great Cosmic body, in which dwells the Divine Consciousness or God, as an incarnation. A world is only a part of an atom. Man is only an infinitesimally tiny atom in the great reaches of Infinity. Man, himself, is made up of tiny atoms in which functions a unit of the Divine Consciousness. All are One in the Great Cosmic scheme of things.

There is a blissful, grand overture of celestial music, of vibrational energy, created by the first and foremost Musician, flowing through all creation, finite and infinite. The organized and beautiful All of reality, the Cosmos, with its many, many singing instruments, can be likened unto one divine symphony orchestra, each instrument with its own key of tonal vibration, and the whole orchestra rendering its particular overall tone frequency of vibratory impulses charged with Cosmic Rhythm. In other words, out there in that starry deep, so seemingly but distance, emptiness and silence, every galaxy, solar system, nebula, sun and planet hums through infinite space under the direction of the Divine Musician, the Supreme Intelligence.

Though there are those instruments slightly off key, striking discordance in the whole, each one is being tuned to its proper keynote through the Great Musician, that the whole may blend in a balanced, harmonious rendition of celestial music—a grand 'Finale' of ordered movement and balance. That glorious heavenly state descends to Earth, and the beauty of peace becomes a reality for mankind.

The very highest octave of Divine Love is resounding upon the Earth. Let your life become a high note of rhythmic harmony, and come to know the beauty of harmony's song. Man must quicken and grow in inner attunement with the Divine Musician's symphonic theme: Eternal Oneness with the Creator.

As for the more serious matters at hand, I am sure there are those among our scientists sincerely and tirelessly working to aid mankind, who seriously realize something of the distressing affairs of Earth that confront man, threatening his very existence. But much information must at present be withheld because of man's incredulity and the public's reaction.

Most of us have either heard about, read about or discussed the subject of fluoridation. It has been circulated that there is high pressure propaganda for fluoridation, by which cities are being fast-talked into unwittingly poisoning their drinking water through use of artificial fluoride, the result of which, it is stated, is semiparalysis or softening of the brain. But the so-called 'rat- poison pushers' cannot outdo Mother Nature. It would be good, common sense to set aside their ruthless fluoridation campaign, and attempt to contrive some means to *purify* poisonous water on a huge scale. The fluoridation conspirators may be able to easily avoid or neutralize their own rat-poison, but not so simply Mother Nature's!

One of Nature's unpleasant changes that our Brothers divulged to me and which man must contend with, is slowly poisoning our fresh water supply. It is a threat to our future safety for in twelve to fifteen years we can be without precious fresh water if our chemists do not discover some way to purify poisonous water or to prevent further contamination.

Climatic changes have been altering the chemical components of the once harmless fluid in the thick skinned pods of the Sargasso sea-weed-like plant, until now it is a deadly poison.

The Sargasso Sea is a gigantic area of tropical seaweed floating endlessly about the ocean currents of the Atlantic Ocean. Terrific change in temperature from cold currents filtering down from fast melting icebergs and glaciers in the Arctic, have produced a chemical reaction. This reaction is stimulated by the salt in the ocean water suddenly turning cold. Freezing water makes the pods brittle. Compressed air inside bursts them open, releasing the poison fluid into the waters.

Poison water is slowly seeping into fresh-water lakes and under ground reservoirs. We cannot count on the ocean absorbing or diluting this poison to the extent that the earth's water supply will be safe for consumption by man, fowl or beast.

Chapter Eleven

ABOARD THE SHIP

For several weeks I felt the presence of someone watching me, and sometimes this feeling disturbed me to no end. I also felt that whoever it could be, they were prevented or not permitted to contact me.

Then one night as I was turning out the lights I was drawn to look out the window. The porch light was burning brightly, flooding the lawn, where stood two small figures, leaning a little forward as if trying to peer in the window. Judging their height by a nearby post, they were not more than four feet three inches tall. They were garbed in brown suits that seemed to be in one piece, and wore some sort of brown hat or cap upon their heads. They reminded me of the legendary Brownies. From the light shining on their faces *they were not the ugly little monsters* so many 'Flying Saucer' reports have maintained. I opened the door and stepped out onto the porch, inquiring, "Can I help you in any way, my friends?" Their only response was to turn and run.

At an ensuing contact with our Brothers and Sisters I mentioned this experience, and was merely told, "Yes, we know about it; they are good people."

It was on this visit that the Brother of Jupiter was wearing a smartly tailored American suit of a beige shade. It was evident he was not accustomed to it and was quite uncomfortable. I asked him, "You are not used to it?" and he admitted, "No, it does not feel well." The two Sisters were wearing skirts and blouses, one dressed in bright pink and salmon-pink shades, the other, yellow-green and blue-green shades, both with matching pumps, the color values blending beautifully.

The three of them indulged a few moments in jesting, bubbling over with zest, apparently entertaining me as I listened amusedly. I was impressed that they wished me to know that they are not always a serious people, but indulge in playful raillery and infectious mirth much as we of Earth do.

Let us go back for a moment to my early mental telepathy contacts. I was given the following information: "There are some who believe that by trying to raise their vibrations, as a group, to a given pitch, we would come in for a contact. Your people must understand it will do little good to send through vibrations to bring us. *They will have to be taught far more than they know now.* Do not try to contact us. We will contact you when the time is right. There is no magnetic power on your planet that can draw our craft in for a landing without our control. We can have landings through thought vibration [telepathy] from one of our planet people on your Earth, or from one of your advanced people of your planet. There must be a specific and important motive."

Now, at this meeting, I inquired if it were true or not that they received and dispatched messages through our radio and infra-red light beams. Our Brother of Jupiter explained, "We observe them but give no attention to them. They are of no value. Others observe them; even your government. If we were to answer signals of such a nature we would include a whole community, but that would result in fear in the minds of many people, which is not our purpose." Later he added that Earth people in using infra-red ray machines may receive sounds from planes of space or the galaxies, and thereby help themselves to gain more knowledge. As for sending messages through our instruments, which utilize artificial power, they would be put out of commission because of the natural power of space that our Brothers use.

It was on this contact the Lady of Pluto, the Brother of Jupiter, and the Lady of Jupiter escorted me to within eight or ten feet of a small majestic craft some sixty feet in diameter. The two ladies mounted the flange of the ship and stood waiting just within the entrance. I had been promised that when the time was right I would be allowed aboard one of their ships. When this would be I did not know, and I was thinking my Brother was dismissing me when he addressed me, saying, "You may go now." As I hesitated he took hold of my arm and, to my surprise, he led me to the ship. It was difficult to believe that this amazing thing was at last happening to me as I walked up the flange and through the open doorway. We entered what could be called a small entrance room, and proceeded through an arched doorway into a rose-lit room neatly furnished with furniture the shape of which is similar to ours, but the material and finish is unlike anything I am familiar with. I could not determine the exact colors due to the rosy light, the source of which was not evident, though the room was evenly lighted. I was permitted to remain but a few minutes, and it was with the greatest reluctance that I departed.

One night several weeks later I felt the urge to look out the window. On raising up on one elbow I saw what I thought to be three stars grouped very closely together. I was wondering how they could appear so close, when they moved, first one, then the other two. Their color changed to yellow-orange. The three moved to a position below the moon where they circled what appeared like a blue-white star. All hung motionless for four or five minutes, then sped away, quickly disappearing. About fifteen minutes later I was contacted via the inner-voice by a Brother who had contacted me some months previously. The vibrations were unusually powerful as they had been before, every word filled with compassion and love and understanding. However, this time I was able to withstand his high thought frequency much better, although I was so overwhelmed the other time that when he left me with his blessings, I beseeched him to come back. I am not ashamed to admit that at that moment I would have given my life to go with him. The nature of these two messages would be non-consequential to my readers. I have also learned there are some things I must retain in the confidence of my memory.

About five weeks more elapsed, and then our Brother of Jupiter came and invited me to accompany him. I was astounded at the sight of the softly glowing, immense, hovering craft we approached which must have been all of four hundred feet in diameter. It loomed before us, a fabulous, gigantic disk with a beveled dome, its magnitude greater than mere words. Either instruments within the ship registered our approach, or else a telepathic message announced us, for when within a dozen steps from it, it tilted so that we took about a twelve inch step up onto the flange. Before leaving, the Captain or Lady of Jupiter informed me, "This large type cruiser [ship] is not up-to-date as others the people of Jupiter have, but it travels interplanetary and even to other solar systems."

As on the smaller ship, we stepped first into an entry room illuminated with a soft light. From here we entered a room wherein the Lady of Jupiter awaited us, seated behind a desk. A lambent, lavender-tinged light filled the room, blending the colors of everything into the same soft, diffused hue, but of lighter and darker shades. Oddly, and also as in the smaller craft, no object cast a shadow, and there was no evidence of the source of light. The walls and ceilings of all rooms had no square corners, but were beveled, and of some shiny, translucent, metal-like material. The floor coverings though firm under the feet, were yet pliable like sponge-rubber. The furniture was designed without square corners or sharp angles. The stand and desk tops of transparent glass-like material, were bereft of any object.

The Lady of Jupiter arose, graciously greeted me, and invited, "We will go to the control room where we will not be disturbed," and added as we proceeded, "The weather is very strange because of your government's experiments. It will be difficult for your people to understand the varying conditions of the weather."

I had taken but a few steps when I noticed a slight, though peculiar feeling in my solar plexus. I gave it little thought at the moment being concerned as to whether I should take a ride at this time or not, should I be invited to go aloft. She perceived my thoughts at once and startled me by disclosing, "It will have to be all right; you are already up two-hundred and seventy thousand feet!"

I was now entering the control room and upon being so informed I stopped, transfixed, a queer sensation hitting me in the pit of my stomach at the thought of being such a height off the ground aboard an alien ship. She sensed my moment of suspense and to dispel it, she calmly reassured me, "You will be all right." I was aware of a slight pressure over my entire body. It lasted but momentarily.

As I turned, amazement was added to shock as I saw that the door I just came through had silently closed, and there remained no sign of a doorway whatever—nothing but the solid wall. As to how the door operated I had not had the presence of mind to notice.

This control room in which I now stood was estimatedly twenty feet by twenty, more or less, and was so arranged as to also serve for the private quarters of the one in charge of the ship. A diffused, misty light pervaded the room. The Lady of Jupiter crossed the room to the far wall where she took a moment to manipulate some controls on the instrument board or control desk, which consisted of rows of button-like levers or switches, some lit up with light. Above the instrument board was a control panel, glowing with a soft light. It appeared to me like a plate-glass window about eight feet long and six feet wide, encasing a series of charts and graphs that operated according to a color-graph system. Never before had I ever seen or heard of anything like it. Lights of different color intensities came and went. These graphs and their flashing color intensities registered and indicated altitude, direction, rate of speed, atmospheric conditions, approaching objects, even to radio and all types of messages transmitted on Earth.

Referring again to the instrument-board, I would say it was possibly ten feet long. In front of this instrument-board, and extended on adjustable arms from below the 'board' itself were three swivel, bucket-like seats with backs that would reach to just below a person's shoulder blades for comfortable back support. Situated at the left end of the 'board', in a tilted position, was a round lens about two feet in diameter. This viewer-lens or observation reflector, was so located that anyone sitting in the bucket-seats could swing them into position so as to clearly observe any projections shown, without getting up from his seat.

At the end of the instrument-board near the viewer-lens was what looked to me to be a round drum-like table, which was so designed that the top reminded me of a wagon wheel or an astrological wheel, the purpose of which was not pointed out to me at this time. However at a later meeting I inquired about it, and my Brother of Jupiter began to elucidate, using words with which I was entirely unfamiliar. Suddenly he hesitated, realizing I did not comprehend such scientific terms. A smile crossed his handsome face, and the Lady of Jupiter interceded, "Kelvin would like to understand it", and continued the topic herself, explaining simply that this particular instrument was employed in locating the position of the craft as they traveled through space, whether they were traveling between planets, systems or galaxies, or within the atmosphere of a planet. At all times this instrument is automatically operating, chart-like disks engaged and disengaged beneath the circular crystal-like top, that map the area of the heavens through which the craft is navigating so that their whereabouts in space, enroute, and destination is instantly determined. Also by pressing lever-like buttons, charts can be inserted of far-off regions of space to which they may be intending to travel. My Brother added that it was not difficult to understand, and that sometime I might be given the opportunity to watch it in operation.

Near the undetectable door through which I had entered the room, was a small stand with crystal-like top. On the wall above and just beyond this stand was a raised, life-like picture, portrayed in natural colors, of a radiant and beautifully transcendental countenance. It seemed so animated with life that I stood spellbound, gazing upon it. It was so like a blend of both, I could not decide whether it was a portrait of a man or woman, nor did it show any age, but was like a reproduction of eternal youth, immortal life, a super-being these Brothers and Sisters highly respected and divinely honored, who meant more to them than anything in their lives. Deeper and deeper whirled my thoughts, until all at once I became aware that in my absorption, I was being impolite to my hostess, and turned in embarrassment to find a strange look of surprise on her comely face, though she did not utter a word. I had beheld their symbol of the Supreme Diety, the source of all things, whom they glorify in every thought and deed.

Upon the wall to the left of the door I had entered was what I shall describe as symbols which reminded me somewhat of Sanskrit writing. These strange symbols extended up and down the wall to within possibly a foot from the floor and the ceiling. Near the center of this portion of the wall was a raised life-size picture of a pair of hands, including a part of the forearms. The hands were not clasped in a handshake or grip, but placed lightly palm to palm.

One portion of the right wall, viewing the room from the door through which I had entered, was a section of panels extending perhaps as high up as eight feet that appeared to me to be cabinet doors. The other portion of the wall was so divided as to look like drawers instead of doors, though neither section was fitted with door knobs or drawer pulls. I can only surmise what lay behind them.

The room, permeated with harmony, was comfortably, elegantly, and uniquely furnished though not lavishly. I doubt there is anything on Earth that would compare with it. The Lady of Jupiter directed me to follow her, and three of us entered a hallway through a door beneath the mural of the hands. After moving forward several feet we turned into a room in which the light was quite dim, and I could not see clearly all that I might have otherwise. There was another Brother present and standing over in the corner by some instruments, but I was not introduced, nor could I see him plainly as in normal light.

I was informed that this large room was where they came for observational purposes. Here a large section of the floor was occupied by a circular, clear magnifying lens around which were several seats. This huge lens drew into plain view scenes below on the Earth or in the atmosphere, which could be projected on a screen on the wall where everything is clear and accurately defined as to detail. The oval-shaped screen appeared to have a depth of six inches and was possibly ten feet long and nearly that high.

I was permitted to look into the huge reflector lens, and to view some of space as it was projected onto the screen. Being in the dark of night with fog below I could only discern the curved outline of the Earth beneath a hazy glow. However, I beheld myriads of dust particles in movement out there in space, reflecting light. Many of these minute points of light changed hues. There were also larger, glowing objects, and some that were dark without illumination. I was given no explanation of what I beheld, other than at some later date I might have the opportunity to see more and have it explained to me. It was not the purpose of this visit aboard to unfold the operation or function of anything I saw.

We returned to the control room and before I knew it we had descended, and were 'hovering' that I might alight. I had felt no sensation of the descent or of coming to a stop. With a heavy heart and a great sadness engulfing me, they bade me farewell until next time. I was back on 'terra firma' physically, but a part of me sailed out into the great beyond with my dear friends aboard the space-craft.

On a future trip into outerspace and at thousands of miles altitude, over 200,000 miles distant, I was invited to view the Earth, which appeared to be about ten feet in diameter, through an optical device which reminds one of an oscilloscope with a graph placed across the screen. Our planet was prefixed in one of the graph sections and showed up much as a pip does, but larger in circumference. From this distance one could not detect any sign of life whatever upon our globe. It hung out there in the midnight-blue blackness of space like a huge yellowish white orb, and emanating a dull, hazy glow. However, at a much greater distance out in space our globe appeared smaller, about four feet in diameter through the optical lens, shedding a sick saffron light against the dark background of space, whereas it should be glowing with brilliant splendor. Viewing it in closer, the unbalance on its axis was scarcely noticeable on the graph, but here at the greater distance away our planet seemed to have taken on a definite additional movement, an angular fluctuating wobble. At no time did I discern the movement we refer to as rotation, only this plainly perceptible staggering like a drunkard. I was quite immersed in, and awed at the sight, and suddenly realizing that this was my world, my home, unstable and wobbling in an alarming manner, I was not in the least bit anxious to return to it.

This then, would in general, portend the significance of our Brother's remark pertaining to more serious matters to contend with than any possibility of a collision with a so-called asteroid. Balance is a fundamental law of the universe, without which worlds leave their courses and all can become confusion. Mankind is governed by the same law of balance; he is the key, the channel, through which a planet maintains balance. This unbalanced condition of our planet is something every man should strive to eliminate. To help establish the balance of Earth on its axis and in its orbit, every human being must endeavor to balance the polarities of his own nature, and raise the state of his consciousness. He must use the knowledge attained in the finite plane as a stepping stone to the point of balance. He will find that deep within the consciousness lies his balance wheel which, if allowed to do so, will work with the finest precision. He must try to remove the low frequency of his thought vibration by replacing desire for power, dominance and destruction with one for order, co-operation and construction, by removing the negative from his life that he now displays in every action. If you could behold your world vacillating on its axis as it is, you would understand better the urgent need for action, for turning within and examining yourself, taking yourself into account, and striving to live the Christ-life, to live in harmony with God's law, with that great and harmonious power that lies behind all. "The work of the world is done by few; God asks that a part be done by you."

In 1954 the director of the institute of meteorics in New Mexico headed a project in which scientists were searching for artificial satellites known to be circling the Earth. Through the magnifying lens I viewed two of these satellites traveling parallel to the Earth's orbit, placed there and controlled by the Guardians of Space. One being farther from the space-craft which I was aboard, appeared smaller, the size of a baseball, the closest one about the size of an indoor ball. They merely looked like small balls of light moving through space, though their radiance was much less than that of our moon when full and bright.

I was told that there was drastic danger of a premature shifting of the Earth's poles, and that these satellites are placed in position around our planet, operating as a medium of counter-balance and to prolong the time of cataclysm, if possible, till the proper cyclic time schedule as appointed by Nature. Long ago man grew away from nature, and we continually and unwittingly attempt to turn the elements against us. The balance of a planet, and the planetary vibration whether positive or negative, are dependent upon the dwellers of a planet. In this instance, our Brothers have had to harmonize their purpose with the workings of nature in order to prevent a premature occurrence that could disrupt the entire solar system. It is highly probable that our already off-balanced condition of Earth could be accelerated by too much radiation released from our bomb-explosions, entirely destroying the Earth's balance in this system, and in turn making space travel dangerous for a long time.

It was the month of December, 1955, when next my Brother and Sister from Jupiter dropped in to see me. I had been planning for my vacation a few weeks away, during which time I intended to travel to Denver, Colorado, meeting my good friend John, flying in from New Jersey, then on to the BROTHERHOOD OF THE WHITE TEMPLE in Sedalia to meet one of the most eminent personages on this Earth I've ever had the good fortune to become acquainted with, and whose identity will become more widely known as this old world reels on into the Time of Trouble. It was not accidental, nor for personal fortune or fame that he quietly established headquarters high in a region of the Rocky Mountain Range. He is working under instruction all the time, *not from some unseen guide* *or spirit*, but by direction of the Great Teachers of the Great White Lodge.* He is indifferent to praise, and desires no personal following. Every word he speaks is spoken from experience and knowledge, and not just something he believes. He demands only loyalty to the Eternal and Divine Consciousness of God!

By my watch it was nine-fifteen p.m. when a flood of soft light descended through the night sky on a wave, then dropped vertically and dimmed out in the vicinity through which I was driving my pick-up truck. I immediately recognized this to be a spacecraft, and brought the car to a stop off the road. I walked out across the stubble of a field toward a faintly luminous object just visible in the darkness. As I drew near I saw the figure of someone outlined in the dim glow of an open door, and was next aware of someone standing by the craft. A mellow, masculine voice from out of the night greeted me. "How are you, my brother?" The Brother of Jupiter advanced silently and clasped my hand in the customary way of greet-

---

* The Great White Lodge is not a legend. It is fully protected, both from the intrusion of man or the forces of nature. Shamballa is the name most often used in referring to the Central Headquarters of the Great White Lodge on Earth. Silently and secretly, unknown to the great mass of people the Great Masters of the Great White Lodge are constantly striving to bring mankind to their own degree of Consciousness. This earthly White Lodge is only a part of a universal or Cosmic White Lodge which has its representatives on every inhabited planet throughout the Cosmos. The retreat of the Cosmic White Lodge is on the star 'Antartes' of the Pleiades, the place which the Bible says is heaven."

ing, while vibrant harmonies of joy coursed through my being. I assured him that I was fine, and we then entered the craft and the presence of the Lady of Jupiter. They imparted to me that they were very busy and could stop but shortly. Without my having mentioned it to them they disclosed they knew of my vacation plans. Noting I was somewhat doubtful regarding my time off from employment, they assured me there was no need to worry; that all would be well. And indeed they were right.

As I returned to the pick-up I paused to watch the craft mount into the night sky and streak across the canopy of the heavens to vanish in the beyond. It was a small ship they came in, probably sixty feet in diameter. They were both attired in neat fitting ski-type suits.

The visit following this one was from the Lady of Pluto, who brought with her two Brothers and a Sister whom I had not met in any former contact. and whom she said I would meet again. They did not indicate what planet they were from. After discussing the necessity of the people of Earth increasing their vibrations to conform in harmony with the vibration of the Earth's orbit, they took their departure, leaving me deeply moved as usual. They came and went in a late model automobile.

Chapter Twelve

FEW ARE CHOSEN

Many of you have interrogated, "Why don't 'they' contact me? Why do they contact him?" One point is significant; our Brothers have contacted people in all walks of life. Position, profession, education, wealth, beauty or homeliness, are not requisites considered in determining whether you are a likely candidate for contact or not. If you are more desirous of being of service, of helping suffering humanity into a condition of greater life than you are of worldly fame or gain, that would be one qualification in your favor. Often a person of little education consumed with the desire for service has a better chance than one of highly evolved intellect who is selfish in his purpose. Too often the academic mind is encumbered by the fetters of education, being a closed channel, not open to the Wisdom of the Divine.

There are certain individuals who are acting as agents for our Brothers, and may well be performing this duty because of some cause set up before entering their present incarnation. The reason a person is contacted goes much deeper than one would ordinarily suspect—to the inner man, *to the nature of the Real You.* If man knew himself, he would know why he is or is not contacted. As is often said, "all that glitters is not gold." The gold tinsel of superficiality is often only a thin veneer covering the darkness of ignorance wherein lies no recognition of the Spiritual Self. One important aim on behalf of the Brothers is to determine whether any designated agent has the courage and profound desire or not, to bring the message of Truth to the people, for too frequently a person will fail because of an inflated ego, or because of criticism and the fear of what others may think or do to him. We are a people impregnated with fear, even afraid of believing in anything at all. However, when one has the Truth and knows it, when he has that conviction, he is not concerned with antagonistic opinions of others or judgment and condemnation passed upon him by skeptics and non-believers. No one's opinions or ridicule ever has or ever will change that which is— Truth, for Truth is Infinite.

'Many are called but few are chosen' because they falter by the wayside and are weak. One must be strong and willing; you can't be half-hearted. It must be understood that God has no preference whatever; He is no respecter of persons for the sun shines alike on all. 'By their works ye shall know them' for each individual has the free and god-given right to choose, and can therefore only be said to be a 'chosen one' because he makes his own choice; he determines his own destiny as he so wills to do good or evil.

God does not send tests to mortals but mortal man tests himself by his own giving in to weakness, by his lack of strength, effort and perseverance. He looks out instead of within. He has not learned to meditate upon himself. When he meditates, he meditates on his pains, worries and troubles, and he immerses himself in them and makes them stronger and more binding. Man is a god but a god bound within the world of Illusion. His body, his mind partakes of this world, yet man has within himself the power to transcend this material earth in which he dwells if he will only learn to know himself.

As long as man is separated from his Spiritual existence, that long he comes under the material law of disorder and inharmony, that long he is bound by conditions and experiences of his environment and life. As long as man is separate from wisdom he is separate from Reality and as long as he is separate from Reality he cannot know himself or God. And when man reaches the state of Universal Consciousness or at-one-ment with God, *there are no divisions, no attributes nor qualities,* nothing but AWARENESS.

I say unto you that within man's own nature lies the key that will release him from bondage, that within man's own nature lies the lock and bar that will fetter him from freedom. Each man, within himself, must use the key. No one may do it for you; only you may do it for yourself.

The time has come when man in this outer, material world must realize that the time is at hand when all the things of chaos and negation are to be broken up, when they are to be reshaped on the potter's wheel and come forth as a perfect vessel and all those who are not so shaped will become the fragments when the vessel is found imperfect.

Other folks query, "What about our government?" Official recognition from the governments of the world and its religious leaders could present the truth of interplanetary visitors coming here in friendship. But as of now the government is reluctant to concede much of any data relative to the presence of interplanetary craft and beings from other planets. It is not so much the governments, but the power behind them that enforces suppression. It is apprehended that once the 'lid is off'—the truth exposed—and people realize the truth of a Greater Way of Life, the present statute of laws could become null and void, meaningless and immaterial to a people who comprehend a righteous freedom that permits of a constructive, positive way of life instead of a destructive, negative one. Remember, nature is free, and man is born in a free state, but he places himself in bondage from birth henceforth by customs, fear, tradition, creeds, religious tenets and legislative laws, dwelling in the darkness of illusion, arguing and reasoning from appearances. The 'lid off' would mean total reconversion, scientifically, politically, religiously, morally, philosophically and economically in every department of national and international life. It would mean a new dispensation, which our established government is not at this time inclined to tolerate. A drastic change is nevertheless due this world of ours for it is to become a place of tranquil peace and concord, of what is real and godly where all men will live together in true brotherhood,* having cast aside the bondage of life to the world of Illusion, and knowing all things as they are in their true and ultimate Reality.

Even now our government could be of extensive recourse to its people in the way of better enlightenment and greater understanding of what actually is. They could throw new light on religions and churches and bibles. It is said there is opposition to the church, and there is a campaign to crush that opposition, to frighten the average man from expressing doubts about the many religious divisions, about church, about God, and about the corporation control of the one-party press. That there are more than 55% of the people of the United States who do not belong to any church or affiliated religious group, and a muzzled press and radio make it virtually impossible for these people to obtain the truth about organized religion,

---

* "True brotherhood always did exist, only man has never realized it. It is not only an ideal to be aspired to, it is a Universal Law, and a fact in nature, for everything in this physical world exists by reason of the mutual helpfulness that all parts render to one another. All beings belong to One Great Brotherhood. It is up to each individual to realize it and live accordingly."

which could not survive in its present form were the truth known. The many labels of religion could be removed and superseded by one standard religion based in its entirety on the teachings taught by Jesus the Christ to his disciples—a teaching as old as antiquity yet in so many ways new to present day man, for he has long been forbidden certain knowledge which he was not yet ready to receive.

The government has in its possession an ancient book or manuscript about which newspapers carried a brief article in the spring of nineteen fifty-five. It was placed in the Congressional Museum for research and study. From it our knowledge of the philosophical and historical foundations of religion could be greatly enriched, and could, with certain other scrolls, have a direct effect on current religious beliefs that would result in a clearer and greater cognizance by the layman of man and his religions.

A revision of school textbooks is greatly needed. Men of science are learning many things they never knew before; they have attained much knowledge which is contrary to old theories propagated and taught by our school systems, but all boards of education in practically all instances refuse to allow anything to be taught that is not printed in the school textbooks. It is imperative that these books be discarded as they are a detriment to our children's education, and serve only to retard the growth both in children and adults, of a better understanding of what actually is, thus slowing the progress of the race. Our public schools are failing to awaken intellectual interest in their students or promote a desire and incentive for greater learning. Our present educational systems are allowing much talent to go largely to waste.

We have spent ten million years in evolutionary progress to rise to the position where we now stand, yet with all we know that past generations did not know, with all we can do that past generations could not do, *we are only now on the threshold of still a greater life* in which we will be literally a different type of race—a superior race. But first the cobwebs of ignorance and superstition must be lifted from the eyes of all people on Earth, and replaced with truth, reason and freedom—freedom from enslavement to negation, to greed, fear, lust, hypocrisy, bigotry, war and destruction. Many preconceived ideas and subversive organizations must be broken down and exposed. We must not allow ourselves to be hampered further by any question of precedents or traditions but rather free ourselves from the outworn traditions and habits of thought, and establish a new method, a new approach to life. True liberty can only come from the understanding of Divine Truth which means a knowledge of the Oneness of God.

There will be those of my readers who will ask, "What are the names of these people from other planets?" During my early mental telepathy contacts I, too, questioned, "Could you please give me your name so I may identify you?" This was the reply, "The names would be many; they are not necessary. Names as your people of Earth use them, are meaningless and but personality. You will know when a change in contact is made; you will feel the difference, and identify us individually by that feeling [conscious consciousness]. If names and identification are given, be very careful for many are false! We do not identify the planets by the appellations your people have applied to them; we know them by orbits. All planets are working together as One with the Creator."

Our perspicacious Brothers and sisters always at all times utilize the greatest of decorum, suitable to time, place, occasion and action. They're able to meet anyone on any level, and do not seem 'queer' for they always adjust themselves to the level of consciousness of the one to whom they are speaking, their speech befitting the character and education of the person of Earth they converse with, no matter his intellectual level or the subject discussed with him. It is true that they know you far better than you know yourself.

No one of them remains on our planet permanently, but only until a mission is fulfilled, sometimes a matter of a few years, and during that time they visit their homes. They care nothing for material glorification or self-aggrandizement, desiring only to use their wisdom to aid mankind and serve the Creator; to help those who have *no* desire for phenomena or selfish desire for power over their fellow man; to help those who unselfishly wish to become more perfect channels for the Christ Consciousness to manifest through.

If an Earth man were transported to a neighboring planet for a visit, in some instances he would need to be acclimatized before reaching his destination as there is some difference between the atmosphere of Earth and that of other planets, though not great. This acclimatization could be accomplished enroute aboard ship, and he would then feel no perceptible difference in the atmosphere upon his arrival. In most cases a native of Earth would be unable to withstand the high spiritual vibration of the people there or the high planetary frequency but for a matter of hours, according to the vibrations of the finite plane on which he functions. That is, the higher he is spiritually the more inured he would be.

However, to my knowledge, it is not possible for an Earthling to live on another planet of higher evolution except under certain conditions, having undergone previous necessary preparations. He would have to be approaching his first degree of Illumination if he has not already become Illuminated, or at least have attained to that state of consciousness wherein he is sincerely striving for spiritual development and studying his spiritual nature as well as material, and applying and putting into operation the knowledge he is gaining. When all planets have been brought into their original harmony of movement man will establish free movement from Earth to other worlds.

And we will find that governments of our neighboring planets consist of a legislative body composed of representatives from every walk of life, and that all problems are solved for the good of all. They do not have a monetary system, but a commodity-service exchange system. They recognize their planet as belonging to the Creator, and share its bountiful supply equally as one large family. Through their knowledge and use of the laws of Nature they have harnessed forces and utilized them in ways that they do not have to spend long hours at work to supply their needs as we of Earth do. Therefore they have ample time for unfolding their abilities, for constructive study, travel and recreation. All planets in our system are represented in what I shall term an interplanetary federation. However, the planet Earth is the only one not openly and willingly participating. It is the sincere hope of our Brothers to bring us into association with the Solar family through knowledge.

To me it is almost an impossibility to surmise the

age of any of these joyous, loving people I have met. As we know time, they are very young looking, having that wonderful bloom of youth, yet being much older than they appear, and rich in wisdom. They once told me I would be greatly surprised if they revealed their age to me, for their age span is one thousand to two thousand years of our Earth time or more. The men have well-built physiques, are immensely good-looking, with clean-cut, regular features; the women with contours ideally proportioned, lissome and lovely, with fine delicate features, coiffures becomingly styled — both sexes truly a beautiful people—a people like nothing but themselves. Their clothes are fashionwise, style and color befitting each personality. Their voices are mellow, finely modulated without any defects such as raspiness, harshness or sharpness so often perceptible in the tonal qualities of Earth people.

Only one time, up until 1956, had I heard a lower-pitched voice, unlike the others, and that, when I was introduced via clairaudience to a Brother from the planet Uranus. He acknowledged, "I am very pleased to meet you. We hope we can contact more people like you on your planet. It would be of great benefit to all." He was aboard a huge carrier-ship with over five-hundred guests from various other planets. At this time I spoke with three others besides this Brother of Uranus. No doubt to ease my disappointment, they owned, "It would be nice if you were here too, but it is not time for you yet. You should not be impatient." And as I have already related my patience and faith, and my efforts to become worthy have been amply rewarded.

Since I was first elevated aloft two-hundred and seventy thousand feet, I have been hurtled at tremendous speed thousand of miles into the far reaches of space to board the gigantic cigar-shaped carriers, to return refreshed and infused with life in spite of the long hours without sleep. My first trip into outer space took place in March, 1956. I left the Earth with two Brothers on a small scout-ship about forty feet in diameter. We traveled an hour and fifteen minutes before arriving aboard a Mother Ship, the likes of which never approaches too closely to this quarantined, prison world. Some of you may think of these trips as pleasure trips, but I affirm that though to me it is the greatest pleasure of my life to be with these dear friends, and privileged to travel in their celestial craft, to be present at a conference or council meeting, and to harken to the wisdom of a Master,* never are

---

* "In reality there is no such thing as a so-called Master. One who has become One with the Divine has not risen above anything. He has merely become one with all things, and in Divine At-one-ment there is no master and servant, only Eternal Oneness. Those we call masters are those who have freed themselves from bondage of negation, and overcome circumstances and things instead of being mastered by them, and he is no different from you or anyone else, only in the matter of development. You have potentially the same powers the Masters have, They, however, are aware of their powers and are able to use them, and you are not."

these trips what we of Earth may consider as pleasure trips, but each a momentous event, always of the gravest import. That having the courage and desire to bring, in the best way I can, the Truth to those of Earth who are ready for the Truth, assisting those in darkness to see the Light, if only a tiny flicker that they may take one step forward, it is adding to the positive growth and harmony of The Whole and the fulfillment of the Creator's great Cosmic Plan. "God's law of cause and effect operates inexorably to the end that all of the jealousies, hatreds, littlenesses and pettinesses of humanity will be distilled and transmuted into Divine Harmony and the Christ Consciousness of God."

I, as many others of this planet Earth, have met, associated with, benefited by, and enjoyed the presence of these highly superior beings from other worlds whose development is inconceivable to people of Earth. We have found them to be shining examples of what we of Earth should be, what we can be, and shall become despite man's solely materialistic minds and egotistical, dominating, destructive nature. Cosmic principles are in the process of transmuting all things on Earth. A new race will emerge in the New Age, for even now a mutation has started taking place in all mankind. Unseen forces are at work throughout the Cosmos, some so subtle even the most sensitive person is not aware of them. Life shall become as it never has been since the Fall of Man, for all darkness and negation shall be dissolved by the Light.

Always in every age and to every people, when the world is in need of spiritual and material leadership, there has come a manifestation of the Christ Consciousness, an Avatar,* who sought to guide man's steps, giving only to man what he made himself ready to receive, and to bring him an understanding of Divine Love which mortal man has spurned for thousands of years. Mankind has wandered far from the fold, and ere all is done, he must be brought back into the fold. "Even though a great change has already taken place countless millions of people throughout the world will be struck dumb when the legions of angels of Heaven** make manifest the glory of the

---

*An Avatar is a world teacher—Lord of the World. He is a soul, which, because it was manifesting on higher planes of consciousness in the beginning, did not partake of the Fall of Man and remained a 'sun' or 'light' of God. An avatar descends only at will to the lower material plane."

**Angels are directing Intelligences. Legions of angels or a host of angels is a spiritual army, not an army that will fight with weapons of destruction but an army of spiritual fire and force, the army of Maitreya, Lord of the World, which will spread over the Earth and conquer negation with spiritual weapons."

"The Bible tells you that Heaven is in the midst of the Pleiades. That is because it is the nucleus of all the spiritual expressions in this world that are working to remove the darkness from man. This center of all spiritual direction is from one of the encircling planets of the star Antartes of the Pleiades."

Divine Presence of the Christ Consciousness." The Creator has decreed a spiritual renaissance and a new era of peace and constructive activities ruled over by the Lord of the World.

"It may seem strange, so many things and so many powers exist without man being aware of them and yet there are many more strange and vast things in the universe that man has no knowledge of," things which have no place in a manuscript such as this, things it would be ineffectual to convey to man when he is not yet ready to receive such knowledge.

Some there are who believe UFO's are the greatest mystery of our century, and though I have assembled the contents of this book somewhat crudely, this notwithstanding, I only hope I have made it clear that there is no mystery connected with them. It is in Knowing that the veil of mystery is lifted. But for all that has been written herein, the fact remains that each individual must at all times be left to follow the dictates of his own inner feelings as to what he shall believe, as to what he shall know and do, for every man has the power of free will. It is rather not for me to deny anyone the choice of making up his mind for himself. For this he must certainly do. No man should be forced into any condition or way of life for man compelled is man in revolt. Therefore, I have set forth these truths that you may so decide. I do not ask that you believe; only that you consider—and if critically, then with an open mind.

Dear reader, whoever you are, a critic, a skeptic, a curiosity seeker, an opponent of Truth, or one of the few seekers of Light and Truth, I have herein revealed to you The Way. The rest is entirely up to you—to chose the way you will travel, to benefit by it or lose by ignoring it, to dedicate your life to the New Spiritual Age, following the Path of Light into the New Kingdom, or to go down in the passing Age of Darkness to be bound at last with Satan. If you believe a year from now what you believe today, the world will have outdistanced you. No one may aid another beyond a certain point. You must desire to help yourself, and do just that. "No man can save a man but himself. Being a god, you are not helpless. You are your Saviour."

It is no unusual trait for "saucer-fans' to eagerly seek and accept any information they can read or hear about UFO's. But there is more to them than just 'flying saucers,' propaganda, phenomena, mystery and sensationalism; their coming heralds a call at the Dawn of the New Age to a New Way of Life. However, when it is confided to Mr. Average Saucer Fan that he now needs to begin to 'know thyself,' his high pitch of interest is diminished; he would rather have his delusions than to make such an effort even though he gain the Truth. Many find it easier to chose the line of least resistance, and go along blindly with the crowds. Verily it has been said that the great mass of mankind has no realization as to where they came from, why they are here or where they are going, either as an individual or as a race of people. It is that we must educate ourselves to think, and not treat our minds carelessly, cramming any old thing into them. Store only that which appertains to the elevation of mind and soul. It takes perseverance to become something else than just an opinionated person.

No doubt there are those of you who will assert that you do 'know yourself.' But let us suppose one of our Brothers confronted you with the question, "What is your purpose in living?" Could you readily answer him, confidently telling him? — "It is my right to serve the Creator by changing disorder into order; it is my purpose to master the condition of negation around me in the material so that I may be free of negative and One with God. Every experience I meet and conquer perfects some of the inharmonious light into a condition of order, and by so doing the Divine Light grows in order.'"

And why should this be your purpose? "It was in the beginning that man was fully aware of his oneness with God, but in a far past cycle, he lost, not God, but his Awareness of his oneness with Him. Man is limited in his concept to the relationship of the world around him, seeing only with his material eyes, realizing only through the medium of his material sense, and therefore his knowledge is bound by the material world in which he lives. The goal of all our seeking is to banish the darkness of ignorance and regain that perfect oneness that is man's true heritage."

Our Brothers infer that, "The Way to true development is a very long road for most people. Many have excellent opportunities to help themselves but they fail because they refuse to study and apply what they learn. If one is persistent, the road is much shorter." There is no longer a middle path—only the right or left. The reason that many students and teachers get lost on The Path is because they will start along one line and only see one thought and concept. The Path can be missed, for too often the Truth is veiled in illusion. Remember, *The Way, The Path* that lies before you is no short and simple one; *it is more than a course of study; it is a way of Life in which each individual applies the underlying Cosmic Laws to his own circumstances and problems according to his understanding.*

To gain knowledge and apply it not and share it not is to do wrong. Above all you will need wisdom— the right use of knowledge. But where are we going to seek knowledge and wisdom? Neither is in books, for books only hold a record of man's search for knowledge and wisdom.

"There is only one eternal and infinite wisdom and knowledge in which there is no variance or turning, and that is found by creating within our own consciousness, even for one instant, the consciousness of Divine Love. In the end knowledge and Divine Love are the same thing."

Fear not an end to the world for there is no such thing as an end to anything—there is only change. However, in many instances we do not realize change. This is because our own ego and body is passing through a process of change that is concurrent with everything around it. Let us take a look at the world.

"For a moment it seems as if everything is quiet. Yet in the undercurrent there is a preparation such as has never gone on before, both by the forces of darkness and the forces of light. Throughout the Middle East the forces, the powers controlled by the anti-christ are moving swiftly in preparation for the great assault by the followers of the Prince of darkness upon the Prince of light and his followers. In all of the countries of the East and of the West the lines of battle have been clearly drawn so far as the forces of the Spiritual Assembly are concerned. But among the material forces it is not yet completely clear upon which side some countries or nations will align themselves nor with what power."

Let there be no mistake, this planet Earth will pass through a few more fateful years, and the hearts of man will be tried and tested as never before. If you remain alive you will see the entire fabric of so-called civilization utterly changed, and a new temporal order arise, based upon the oneness of mankind in co-operative freedom. The foundation stones have already been laid, and a tremendous task lies ahead. You have a task to do if you are moving in the Christ Consciousness. It is not work. To be a part of the great task of bringing about the Christ Kingdom on Earth and the Brotherhood of Man, is a pleasure. How true the words of our Brothers when they stated there is much studying to be done and much work to do. "Yet greater before ye is work to be done."

A new era in living lies ahead in which a state of all things we have held as material value will pass away. Every individual is now confronted with the necessity of becoming adjusted to living in a Spiritual Age under a coming new dispensation. It is that you should be prepared lest we be a people defenseless against the evil forces of the anti-christ, who works in many and strange ways, and employs attractive disguises polka-dotted with peace-talk, logic, idealism, and bits of truth for bait. It is that you should place your spiritual house in order for whatever may come as we are in a great crisis period. It is true that for a long time we have given our attention entirely to the gaining of material things rather than spiritual things, and habits once formed are difficult to break. But you should start now, right where you are, and from that worthy place never turn back no matter how stormy or difficult The Way. You cannot afford to wait for the other fellow to do it for you while you sit back on your laurels, for each individual has his own task to perform, a part to play that no one else can do for him.

A foundation on the material plane is the first step in the great search for life, light and love. No matter what comes, live as though you are going to live forever, for the body is the temple of the eternal, living soul, designed in the first place in order for the Infinite to manifest in the material. Endeavor to train the mind's eye to see beyond the physical world of concrete things that unbelief may be overcome and the veil rent. Rise to the spiritual heights of the mountain top where your view is unlimited by the atmosphere of the mortal in the valley below!

Refrain from clinging to that which fetters and binds, and falter not in your sincerity as a seeker of Truth. You should leave no stone unturned in this quest. Think not of Truth as an abstract thing since in reality it is something to be lived each day. "There are Teachers and Masters on your planet," our Brothers assured me, "who would love to lead your people into Truth, to guide them in the way through which they could come to know the laws which regulate the Cosmos and learn to live in harmony with their purpose. They are very fortunate to have as their resource in learning Truth, access to one of the finest Teachers on your planet."

Making your first objective the attainment of Truth, strive for a clear and detailed understanding of man, his life and his relationship to his fellow men, to the Creator, the world and Universe in which he lives and has his being, and how he fits into the Divine Plan of Creation. Make your goal the Awareness of your Oneness with the Creator, united in purity of purpose and as one with the great Cosmic Progression. Open your hearts to your fellow men from other worlds, and let the breath of peace and freedom carried on the great space-ways of the Cosmos, sweep through your souls. Harken to The Call of the New Dawn of the Cosmic Age! Begin now to 'know thyself' that you may become a Warrior of the Dawn!*

---
* Warrior of the Dawn: disciple; Divine channel of the New Age. Warrior of the teaching of Truth.

ADDENDA

Symbolism of the Great Seal of the U. S.

and

The Great American Eagle

There is found in symbolism a universal language translatable by any individual of any race if he has a requisite knowledge of Universal Law. If one desires to know the realities of God and of man, he should learn to read the sign language of symbols, of both human and divine creation. Symbolism has been utilized throughout the ages for the purpose of concealing the secret Ancient Wisdom from the unworthy. Being the most fundamental language of hidden truths, symbolism was introduced into our national life. The destiny of America is indicated by symbols which are circulating in the hands of the American people throughout the device of money displayed in the actions of everyday life. We unsuspectingly pass this legal tender from hand to hand without a second thought, and without considering for an instant the truths embedded in the symbolism.

The most important of these symbols is the Great Seal of the United States. The design for the obverse side as well as the reverse side of the seal appears on the back of our Dollar bills. It was not until 1935 that the reverse side was cast into a die and used. We are quite familiar with the emblematic figures of the eagle and the olive branch, the stars and the motto used on our silver dollars since the beginning. As America holds the future of the world in her hands, the symbolism of the Greal Seal and the American Eagle are of interest to every citizen of the United States. Symbols being keys to doorways leading to truths, this book would be incomplete without excerpts from The Symbolism of the Great Seal of the U. S. and The Great American Eagle by M. Doreal. "This information will be especially interesting to those who have wondered about the outcome of the present world conditions and the future of the American people."

There is much evidence that the founders of our nation were inspired by their vision of a Golden Age in which infinite justice would rule, and from this vision formed a governmental plan to serve as a foundation upon which a higher civilization could materialize. The vision which the founders of the nation saw has been aptly recorded in the symbols of the Seal. The time is now propitious for the American people to see again the vision which played such an important part in the formation of our government. Therefore, in due humility, we present this vision as it may be read in the symbol of the Great Seal of the United States.

Soon after the war, Benjamin Franklin, John Adams and Thomas Jefferson were appointed as a committee to prepare a Great Seal for the new republic and they employed a French West Indian, De Simitiere, to furnish the design and also sketch any designs suggested by the committee. A number of proposed designs were suggested, but for some reason or other were rejected. After vainly trying to perfect a seal which would meet with the approval of Congress, Thomson, Secretary of Congress, finally received from John Adams, then in London, a simple and appropriate device, suggested by Sir John Prestwich, who was a warm friend of America and an accomplished antiquarian. It met with approval, and in June 1782 was adopted as the Great Seal. Leaving out all reference to symbolism it may be described thus:

The obverse side consists of an escutcheon with thirteen stripes, red, white and blue, spangled with thirteen stars placed on the breast of an American eagle without support to denote self-reliance. On the eagle's beak a scroll with the words, "E Pluribus Unum." As a crest over the head of the eagle a golden glory breaking through a blue cloud with thirteen golden stars. In its right talon an olive branch and in its left thirteen arrows.

On the reverse side is a pyramid unfinished; in the zenith an eye in a triangle, surrounded with a glory, over the eye the words, "Annuit Coeptis (God has favored the undertaking). On the base of the pyramid the Roman letters MDCCLXXVI (1776) and underneath, the motto, "Novus Ordo Seclorum" (A new order of the ages.)

The American eagle is a bird peculiar to this continent and therefore showed what country the seal was speaking of. The eagle, with its wings spread, is the messenger between Earth and

Heaven, carrying the prayers of the new nation to the cloud of glory, representing God. In its left talon is an olive branch representing the peace desired by the nation, but in the right talon is a bundle of thirteen arrows representing the forces and powers of protection of Jesus and the twelve.

The Shield with the thirteen stripes represented the thirteen colonies, the protection of America. The stripes not only meant the thirteen original states, but also Jesus and the twelve disciples who acted as a shield to the states, which had been formed in the name of God.

The Cloud of Glory represents a fulfillment of prophecy. The thirteen stars on a blue field with a golden glory breaking through a cloud, show the light of God shining through the thirteen representatives of God (Jesus and the twelve apostles) upon the eagle bearing the shield.

The scroll inscribed, "In God We Trust," in the eagle's beak represents the power of God, which the new nation believed protected and upheld them. On the reverse side the unfinished pyramid represents the unfinished nation which was dedicated to God, and which under the eye in a triangle and surrounded by the glory, would eventually result in a new perfected Age. On the base of the pyramid the words, "Novus Ordo Seclorum," (A new order of the ages) signifies the beginning of a new period in the manifestation of man.

The eye represents the All-seeing eye of the Godman, which would be opened in the new age when the pyramid had been completed by the triangle or unit of the body, mind and soul of the nation. When the eye is open the glory or light of God shines through man.

The most vital symbol to us now is the unfinished pyramid of thirteen steps or stages. In the original design it was intended for thirteen stones to be shown in each step. If we multiply thirteen by thirteen (or thirteen steps by thirteen original states) we have one-hundred and sixty-nine. The beginning of this nation was 1776; add 169 to 1776 and we have 1945, the year when this nation reached as high as it could go under the old order. America has been confronted with grave decisions. On the outcome rests the fate of the nation. It will either fall into oblivion through materialism or ascend to the triangle suspended above in which shines the Light of The Ancient One, the Ancient of Days. If this happens then a great spiritual nation will be evolved to lead the rest of the world from the darkness of negation into which it will have fallen.

Each and every one can do their part to bring about the descent of the Great Spiritual Light. Let us go forward, strong in the faith of our founders, that America and her principles shall survive.

THE GREAT AMERICAN EAGLE was chosen to represent the formation of our democratic life. In the Ancient legends the eagle is the material representative of the spiritual bird, the Phoenix, the symbol of Immortal Life. In the Great Seal of the United States of America we find the eagle representing this life, as the carrier of the banners of Peace, Power, Unity and Liberty into the Age of Universal Happiness.

The spreading wings of the eagle represent the life of the American Spirit. They are so shown to represent that the sole purpose of the eagle is, that it shall fly, when the proper time comes, from the old order into a new.

The eagle wears an escutcheoned shield, upon which is the insignia of his new birth. The thirteen bars on the shield represents the thirteen Original Colonies, and in their Union the life of the eagle began.

In the eagle's right claw is shown an olive branch, a symbol of peace, which he holds as a power in the world that the Spirit of Life might grow. In his left claw he clasps a bunch of arrows, a symbol of power in war, which he wields to protect the weak that they might grow and become strong. There are thirteen arrows and thirteen leaves on the olive branch, thus showing there will be thirteen times thirteen periods (years) of time in which the New Republic must grow before entering into the Greater Life.

The nine feathers in the eagle's tail represent the formulative principle of creation, and the white head the spiritual intelligence which shall guide the Republic through the thirteen stages of its growth and preparation for the Spiritual Kingdom; shown as a heavenly Glory above the eagle's head.

The scroll inscribed, "In God We Trust," in the eagle's beak, represents by whose power, it was believed, that the nation was formed and would be protected.

The eagle's head is turned to the right toward the cardinal direction of the midday sun. The eagle is thus shown with his wings spread, ready to fly when the sun reaches the meridian.

The Cloud of Glory of thirteen Golden stars, with twelve forming an interlaced triangle around the thirteenth, resembles the Great Seal of Solomon.

It has been said that this represents the equilibrium of the Macrocosmic and Microcosmic worlds of creation within an infinite circle. We can see within this brilliantly illumined cloud the promised Christ-Kingdom of twelve states centered around one head.

It is curious to note how often the number thirteen appears as an important part in this symbolism. It is evident that the number thirteen must contain some spiritual relation to the order and movement of the Universe. We observe that Jesus had twelve disciples, forming thirteen; Odin brought twelve priests or gods to Europe from Asia. There were twelve stones in the breast-plate of the high-priest of Israel, the stones and plate forming thirteen; the twelve houses of the zodiac controlled by the sun, forming again the number thirteen. Many more could be cited but these are sufficient to suggest the Mystic thirteen which had a significant part in the forming of the U.S.A.

Now, having learned something of the meaning of these symbols, we may reconstruct the vision as it is represented by the symbols of the Great American Seal and read its message in the following manner:

From the ashes of the Immortal Phoenix* there appeared a baby eagle. Thirteen twigs were collected together to form the eagle's nest. And in the warmth of the morning sun the eagle thrives and becomes strong, and the twigs become a sturdy tree of many branches. And when the sun arrives at the meridian, the Immortal Spirit will be revived and the eagle will fly into the Sun.

---

* "In the symbol of the phoenix arising from its ashes we find the symbol of the Cosmic Egg." It is also known as the symbol of regeneration.

WHAT THE BROTHERHOOD OF THE WHITE TEMPLE TEACHES

It teaches you how to KNOW the causes behind all effects.

It teaches you how to use the laws of health and long life.

It teaches that there is nothing supernatural; that everything is natural and operates according to fixed laws.

It takes away the veil of mystery from the hidden things of life and reveals them as they are.

It solves the mysteries of life and death, teaching what each is.

It directs you along the path of light, so that you will eventually find the master within, and become an illuminated Sun of God.

The Brotherhood teaches the fundamental and natural laws of the Universe and how to operate them, so that life, light, and power become the NATURAL THINGS in your life.

MATERIAL RECOMMENDED FOR YOUR PERUSAL

Flying Saucers Have Landed . Leslie and Adamski
Inside the Space Ships . George Adamski
Flying Saucers . . . . M. Doreal
The White Sands Incident
Steps to the Stars . . . . Daniel Fry
Aboard a Flying Saucer . . . Truman Bethurum
My First 10,000,000 Sponsors
Strangest of All . . . . . . Frank Edwards
Roof of the World (Tibet) . Amaury De Reincourt
Brotherhood of Mount Shasta (novel) Eugene Thomas
Reincarnation for Every Man . . Shaw Desmond
Training and Work of an Initiate . Dion Fortune
Lo!
The Book of the Damned
Wild Talents
New Lands . . . . Charles Fort
The Lost Continent of Mu
The Sacred Symbols of Mu
Cosmic Forces of Mu . . . James Churchward
Flying Saucer Conspiracy . . Donald E. Keyhoe
I Rode a Flying Saucer
"Proceedings" (First 4 Volumes) . George Van Tassel

ANCIENT WISDOM

The Brotherhood teaches by correspondence all the Secret Wisdom of the Ancients. Its college gives the Degree of Doctor of Metaphysics on completion of the course. Its headquarters is high in the Rocky Mountains on nearly 2000 acres—its printing plant, office, Temple and some eighty homes occupied by members as well as dormitories and administration building are assurance of a permanent organization. Regular lectures and classes are conducted here the year round for residence members, in addition to the correspondence lessons which are sent all over the world. You are invited to write for free literature comprising "Master Your Destiny", our magazine "Light On the Path" now in its 21st year of publication, a picture folder and a copy of our weekly Truth Sheet—no obligation.

Little Temple Library Books
50c each; 12 for $5.00

Each comprises an hour to an hour and a half lecture by Doreal, founder of the Brotherhood

- Astro-Chemical Analysis
- The Authentic St. Germain
- Symbolism of the Life of Jesus
- Symbolism of the Great Seal of the U. S.
- Science of Health
- Soul Cycles
- Ancient America
- The Banner of Shamballa
- Mystery of the Moon
- Divine Healing
- The Akashic Records and How to Read Them
- Polar Paradise
- Mysteries of Mt. Shasta
- The Inner Earth
- Mysteries of the Gobi
- Atlantis and Lemuria
- Christ and the Last Days
- The Pineal Eye
- The Perfect Way
- Personal Magnetism
- Man and the Mystic Universe

- The Occult Anatomy of Man
- Tibet and its Religion
- Astral Projection and How to Accomplish It
- Concentration and Relaxation
- The Master Key
- Shamballa, or the Great White Lodge
- Webs of Destiny
- The Dream State
- Light and Color
- The Wheel of Life
- Material Inharmony and How to Overcome It
- The Secret of True Prayer
- Treasures of Light
- Dragons of Wisdom
- Milarepa, The Tibetan Saint
- The Great Masters of the Himalayas
- The Spinal Brain and Health
- Some Previous Incarnations of Jesus and the Unknown Period of His Life
- How to Live in Harmony With Divine Law
- Mystery Teachings of the Second Coming of Christ
- Bardo, the Journey of the Soul After Death
- Wisdom of the Kabbala
- Many That Are Now Living Shall Never Die
- The Return of the Gods to America
- Man's Higher Self, His Subtle Bodies—How They Influence His Life
- Secret Teachings of the Himalayan Gurus
- The Ten Lost Tribes of Israel
- The Secret Teachings of Jesus
- Reincarnation, Life After Death
- Maitreya, Lord of the World
- The Soul and Its Nature
- The New Religion
- Adam and the Pre-Adamites
- The Great Temple
- The Dweller on the Threshold
- Creation and the Fall of Man
- Mysteries of the Mayas

THE BROTHERHOOD OF THE WHITE TEMPLE
Sedalia, Colorado

www.ingramcontent.com/pod-product-compliance
Lightning Source LLC
Chambersburg PA
CBHW072128160426
43197CB00012B/2035